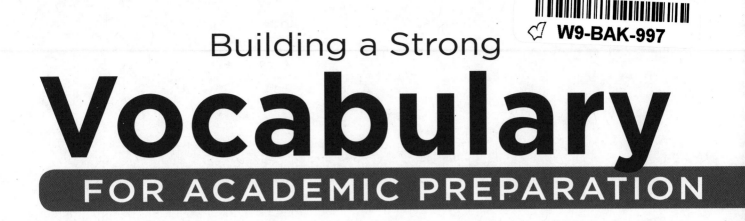

Building a Strong
Vocabulary
FOR ACADEMIC PREPARATION

Ellen Northcutt

Christine Griffith Wagner

New Readers Press
ProLiteracy's publishing division

Building a Strong Vocabulary for Academic Preparation
ISBN 978-1-56420-899-6

Copyright © 2016 New Readers Press
New Readers Press
ProLiteracy's Publishing Division
101 Wyoming Street, Syracuse, New York 13204
www.newreaderspress.com

All rights reserved. No part of this book may be reproduced or transmitted in any form or by any means, electronic or mechanical, including photocopying, recording, or by any information storage and retrieval system, without permission in writing from the publisher.

Printed in the United States of America
10 9 8 7 6 5

Proceeds from the sale of New Readers Press materials support professional development, training, and technical assistance programs of ProLiteracy that benefit local literacy programs in the U.S. and around the globe.

Editor: Beth Oddy
Editorial Director: Terrie Lipke
Designer: Cathi Miller
Technology Specialist: Maryellen Casey

CONTENTS

To the Learner **5**

UNIT 1 Social Studies: Lewis and Clark . . . . **.8**

Exercise 4: Prefix *pro–* 11

Exercise 5: Root *spec* 11

UNIT 2 Social Studies: The Civil War **16**

Exercise 4: Prefix *uni–*. 19

Exercise 5: Roots *cede, ceed, cess*. 19

UNIT 3 Social Studies: Immigration . . . . **.24**

Exercise 4: Prefix *anti–* 27

Exercise 5: Root *migr* 27

UNIT 4 Social Studies: The 19th Amendment . . . . **.32**

Exercise 4: Roots *mand, mend*. 35

Exercise 5: Suffixes *–ion, –tion, –ation*. 35

UNIT 5 Social Studies: The Great Depression **40**

Exercise 4: Root *press* 43

Exercise 5: Suffix *–ment* 43

UNIT 6 Social Studies: Hoover Dam. **48**

Exercise 4: Prefix *mid–* 51

Exercise 5: Suffixes *–able, –ible* 51

UNIT 7 Science: Ecosystems. **56**

Exercise 4: Suffixes *–logy, –logist* 59

Exercise 5: Suffix *–al* 59

UNIT 8 Science: Animal Behavior. **64**

    Exercise 4: Prefixes *co–, com–, con–* 67

    Exercise 5: Roots *act, ag* .67

UNIT 9 Science: Earth's Changing Surface **72**

    Exercise 4: Prefix *ex–* 75

    Exercise 5: Suffix *–ive* 75

UNIT 10 Science: Natural Disasters **80**

    Exercise 4: Roots *vid, vis* .83

    Exercise 5: Suffix *–ity* 83

UNIT 11 Science: Climate Cycles and Change **88**

    Exercise 4: Prefixes *circ–, circum–* 91

    Exercise 5: Suffix *–ic* 91

UNIT 12 Science: Space. **96**

    Exercise 4: Prefix *trans–* .99

    Exercise 5: Roots *astr, aster* 99

Answer Key **104**

Appendices **109**

    I: Common Prefixes 109

    II: Common Suffixes. 110

    III: Common Roots 111

    Personal Dictionary 112

TO THE LEARNER

Building a Strong Vocabulary for Academic Preparation

This book will help you build the vocabulary and vocabulary skills you need to succeed at school and on academic tests.

This is a list of the topics in the book. Which of these things do you know something about or are you interested in?

Check YES or NO.

YES	NO	
		Lewis and Clark
		The Civil War
		Immigration
		The 19th Amendment
		The Great Depression
		Hoover Dam
		Ecosystems
		Animal Behavior
		Earth's Changing Surface
		Natural Disasters
		Climate Cycles and Change
		Space

As you work through this book, you will learn many ways to recognize, understand, and use words in social studies and science contexts.

© New Readers Press. All rights reserved.

About *Building a Strong Vocabulary for Academic Preparation*

THE UNITS

There are 12 units in this book. A unit begins with two readings; each has seven boldfaced vocabulary words. One of each set of words is identified as "Functional Vocabulary;" these words are commonly used in classrooms and on tests, so they are especially useful to know. You'll see the vocabulary words throughout the unit. You'll get lots of practice defining and using them.

VOCABULARY STRATEGIES

You'll also learn strategies you can use to build your vocabulary. These strategies will improve your reading and writing skills as well. And that will help you at home, in your community, at work, and at school.

Word Parts

You will learn about breaking words into parts, including prefixes, suffixes, and roots. When you know the meanings of a word's parts, you can often figure out the new word's meaning.

Context

Did you know that most readings contain clues that can help you figure out an unfamiliar word? These are called context clues. You will learn how to look for different kinds of clues, such as synonyms, antonyms, examples, and definitions. You will also practice using clues to choose the meaning of a word.

Dictionary and Parts of Speech

A dictionary is a great resource when you want to build vocabulary. You can use a dictionary to find a word's pronunciation, to understand what parts of speech a word can play, and to learn a word's meanings. Many activities in this book will ask you to use a dictionary to understand different parts of speech and to choose the correct meaning of a word.

Multiple Meanings

Many words in English can have more than one meaning. You will practice figuring out the correct meanings of words by thinking about their contexts and how they are used in sentences.

FEATURES

Exercises

Practice is the best way to learn something new. So each unit has lots of activities to develop your new vocabulary and vocabulary strategies. The more you do, the more you'll learn and remember. Research shows that people learn new vocabulary when they see words several times and practice using the words in different ways.

© New Readers Press. All rights reserved.

Tips

Tips appear on the sides of many pages. You'll find helpful hints there. Some tips give information about specific words, such as how to say or spell them. Others identify strategies that you can use to figure out word meanings. Read the tips before you do the exercises. They can help you to complete the work and develop your vocabulary skills.

Testing Tips

Tests are a big part of your life as a student. The advice in this section will help you succeed in class as well as give you strategies for answering test questions.

Personalization Activities

Many pages include questions for you to answer using your own experience, ideas, and knowledge. There are no right or wrong answers to these questions. Asking and answering personal questions is an excellent way to practice and remember new words. You will develop your writing, speaking, and listening skills as you complete these activities.

Answer Key and Word Part Lists

You can check your answers by looking in the Answer Key at the back of this book. You will also find lists of common prefixes, suffixes, and roots there. These lists will be good resources even after you finish the book.

Personal Dictionary

Use the Personal Dictionary on page 112 to keep track of new words you want to remember.

SETTING GOALS

Many students define their success in school by setting and meeting goals. A goal is something you want to achieve. You may have a goal for using this book. Maybe you want to be a better reader. Maybe you want to get a better job. Maybe you want to pass a test or do better in school.

Complete this sentence:

I'm using this book because I want to _____

_____

Review this page every few weeks. You may find that you need or want to revise your goal.

© New Readers Press. All rights reserved.

1 Lewis and Clark

VOCABULARY

Read these words from the passage. Check the words you know.

- [ ] acquired
- [ ] continent
- [ ] expedition
- [ ] explore
- [ ] prepare
- [ ] territory

Functional Vocabulary

- [ ] identify

The Louisiana Purchase

After the U.S. **acquired** a huge piece of land in 1803, Meriwether Lewis and William Clark led a famous **expedition** to study it.

In 1803, President Thomas Jefferson arranged to buy from France an 828,000-square-mile band of land along the U.S. western border. Known as the Louisiana Purchase, the area stretched from the Mississippi River to the Rocky Mountains. The newly purchased **territory** doubled the size of the United States.

The government hired Meriwether Lewis and William Clark to **explore** the land west of the Mississippi River. The main purpose of their expedition was to find a water route across the **continent** to the Pacific Ocean. Jefferson thought this could help make future trade easier. Other purposes of the trip were to **identify** and study plants and animals in the territory, make maps, and set up trade with and learn about American Indians.

To **prepare** for the trip, Lewis took courses in medicine, zoology (the study of animals), and botany (the study of plants). He studied maps and journals of trappers and traders. Clark was good with boats and was an excellent mapmaker. He oversaw the building of the expedition's 55-foot long boat. Lewis and Clark got other smaller boats, a crew, and supplies ready. The group was called the Corps of Discovery. Their adventure began on May 14, 1804, and lasted for more than two years. They traveled more than 8,000 miles.

1. Vocabulary Focus

Complete each sentence with a word from the vocabulary list.

1. When you _____ for something, you get ready.

2. If you bought something, you _____ it.

3. A _____ is one of the large landmasses on Earth.

4. When people take a trip with others to study or learn about a place, they are part of an _____.

5. When you _____ an area, you travel there to learn about it.

6. When you _____ something, you recognize it and say what it is.

7. A _____ is a part of a country that is not yet given the full rights of a state.

© New Readers Press. All rights reserved.

Discoveries

Lewis and Clark's expedition greatly increased knowledge of the American West and later inspired many people to move westward.

In 1803, little was known about the lands west of the Mississippi River. Maps **labeled** much of the area as "unknown," and some showed California as an island. Books of the time **described** erupting volcanoes and mountains of salt in the **region**. Some people imagined that animals like seven-foot-tall beavers, unicorns, and woolly mammoths lived there.

President Jefferson instructed the explorers to record "the face of the country." During the **journey**, Lewis and Clark wrote daily about what they saw. As they traveled, they drew maps and recorded **observations** of the stars and the **geography** of the land. Jefferson directed them to collect information about the American Indians they met, many of whom provided important support to the expedition.

The explorers also studied the plants and animals that they encountered. They described 120 kinds of animals, including grizzly bears, buffalo, and prairie dogs, as well as almost 200 kinds of plants. They also shipped **specimens** back, including five live ones. One, a prairie dog, even lived out its life at the White House.

2. Vocabulary Focus

Write the word from the vocabulary list that means that same thing as the underlined word or words.

_____ 1. Lewis and Clark's team collected <u>samples</u> of new kinds of plants they saw.

_____ 2. They wrote down <u>notes and comments</u> about the land and rivers.

_____ 3. The explorers <u>recorded details about</u> the land, plants, animals, and people they saw.

_____ 4. In the early 1800s, maps did not have many details about the <u>natural features</u> of the West.

_____ 5. Their <u>trip</u> started near St. Louis, Missouri, on May 14, 1804.

_____ 6. Lewis and Clark <u>wrote information on</u> maps with the locations of waterfalls and river rapids.

_____ 7. Parts of the <u>area</u> Lewis and Clark explored were mountainous.

© New Readers Press. All rights reserved.

VOCABULARY

Read these words from the passage. Check the words you know.

- [ ] described
- [ ] geography
- [ ] journey
- [ ] labeled
- [ ] region
- [ ] specimens

Functional Vocabulary

- [ ] observations

3. Work With New Vocabulary

Write T *if the statement is true. Write* F *if the statement is false and explain why it is false.*

1. _____ If you study **geography**, you study people's languages, cultures, and traditions.

   _____

2. _____ A person can walk across a **continent** in a day.

   _____

The letter *c* in *specimen* makes the *s* sound.

3. _____ You cannot see or touch a **specimen**.

   _____

4. _____ A **territory** is a part of a country that is not a full state.

   _____

5. _____ A **journey** is a short, easy trip that you take every day.

   _____

6. _____ When you **label** something, you write information on it.

   _____

7. _____ If you write down your **observations**, you write about things you feel or imagine.

   _____

Answer the questions. Explain your answers.

Words that end in *–fy* are verbs. Do you know the words *simplify, liquefy, notify*?

8. What are some ways that people can **identify** you?

   _____

9. What **region** of the country do you live in? How would you **describe** it?

   _____

10. How would you **prepare** for a social studies test?

    _____

11. Who would you take on an **expedition** to **explore** another planet? Why?

    _____

12. What are some ways that countries **acquired** land in the past?

    _____

© New Readers Press. All rights reserved.

4. Prefix *pro-*

The prefix *pro-* can mean "in front of; before; for; forward." This prefix is usually added to roots that are not words. For example, in the word *provide*, the prefix *pro-* is combined with *vide*, which is a root but not a word.

Choose a word from the list to complete each sentence. If you aren't sure of a word's meaning, look it up in the dictionary.

proceed	procure	produced	protect	provided

1. Lewis and Clark had to _____ a lot of supplies, including guns, food, and tools, before the trip.

2. Lewis's dog, Seaman, helped _____ the expedition from animal attacks.

3. Congress _____ the expedition with $2,500 to spend on goods and supplies.

4. In 1805, Lewis wrote in his journal that the group was excited and ready to _____ with the journey after spending the winter at Fort Mandan.

5. Film director Ken Burns _____ a film series about Lewis and Clark in 1997.

Write your own sentences with these words that begin with pro.

6. problem: _____

7. prohibit: _____

> The prefix *pro-* can also mean "in favor of; supporting." For example, *pro-American*; *pro-reform*. In these examples, pro and a hyphen are added to whole words, not to the roots of words.

5. Root *spec*

A root is the base unit in a word. Roots can be combined with other roots, prefixes, and suffixes to form words. The root *spec* means "to look; to watch." For example, a *spectator* is a person who watches an event.

Match each word to its definition. Write the letter of the correct definition on the line.

_____ 1. speculate   a. to look at something carefully

_____ 2. inspect   b. to look up to someone

_____ 3. specific   c. clearly defined

_____ 4. perspective   d. something that is amazing to see or look at

_____ 5. respect   e. to think about a topic and make guesses about it

_____ 6. spectacle   f. a way of looking at something

> The roots of many English words come from Greek and Latin. Learning common roots can help you break words into parts to figure out meanings.

© New Readers Press. All rights reserved.

6. Context Clues: Synonyms and General Clues

You can use general clues such as the topic you are reading about and a word's part of speech to figure out the word's meaning.

When you don't understand a word that you have read, you can use context to figure out the meaning. The context is the words and sentences surrounding the word.

Read the paragraph. Look for clues to help you understand the meanings of the boldfaced words. Write definitions on the lines.

Lewis and Clark's main **mission** was to find a water route to the Pacific Ocean. But another **purpose** or reason for the trip was to learn about the American Indians living in the area. During their journey, the explorers **encountered** about 55 **tribes**, or cultural groups of American Indians. Some groups that they met were friendly, while others were fearful and **hostile**. Without the help of American Indians, the Corps of Discovery most likely would have **starved** to death or become lost crossing the continent.

The word *corps* is pronounced the same as *core*. The *p* and *s* in *corps* are silent.

1. A **mission** is _____

2. A **purpose** is _____

3. When you **encounter** something, you _____

4. A **tribe** is _____

5. When people are **hostile**, they are _____

6. If you **starve**, you _____

Words like *also, as, like, likewise, similar to,* and *same* can sometimes be clues that an author is using synonyms.

When you read an unfamiliar word, look for a synonym to help you figure out the meaning. Synonyms are words with the same or nearly the same meaning.

Look for a synonym to help you understand the meaning of each boldfaced word. Underline the synonyms you find.

7. Meriwether Lewis made lists of the **provisions** needed for the trip. These supplies included guns, scientific instruments, writing supplies, and gifts for American Indians.

8. Lewis **preserved** plant specimens. He saved their stems, leaves, and flowers and pressed them flat so they could be studied later.

9. President Jefferson **appointed** Lewis to lead the Corps of Discovery. Then Lewis chose William Clark to help him lead.

10. Lewis and Clark's journals describe an **abundance** of buffalo. Clark recorded seeing large numbers of the animals, as many as 10,000 at a time.

© New Readers Press. All rights reserved.

7. Parts of Speech and the Dictionary

A word can play more than one part in speech. For example, the word *piece* **can be a noun that means "a part of something." It can also be a verb that means "to put together." To find the correct definition in the dictionary, first figure out the word's part of speech.**

Write the part of speech of each boldfaced word on the short line. Then look up the word in a dictionary and write the definition that matches how the word is used in the sentence.

1. The list of **supplies** included more than 10 pounds of fishing hooks and line.

   _____ _____

2. Lewis and Clark were looking for a **direct** water route to the Pacific Ocean.

   _____ _____

3. Lewis and Clark shipped many specimens back during their journey, including several **live** ones.

   _____ _____

4. Lewis thought that gift-giving and **trade** were important to most American Indians.

   _____ _____

5. The mountains **stretch** as far as the eye can see.

   _____ _____

> A dictionary will list the part of speech next to each entry word. Most dictionaries use these abbreviations:
>
> n = noun
> v = verb
> adj = adjective
> adv = adverb

> The pronunciation of *live* depends on the part of speech. When *live* is an adjective, it rhymes with *five*. When it is a verb, it rhymes with *give*.

8. Multiple-Meaning Words

Words can have more than one meaning or definition. To figure out the correct meaning, look at the context of the sentence.

Look at each underlined word. Circle the letter of the best definition.

1. Lewis and Clark <u>arranged</u> to get horses from the Shoshone Indians.
   a. put things in order
   b. planned ahead of time

2. The main <u>object</u> of Lewis and Clark's trip was to explore the Missouri River and find a way to the Pacific Ocean.
   a. an aim or goal
   b. a thing you can see and touch that is not alive

3. Today, travelers can follow the same <u>route</u> the explorers took.
   a. a way that you follow to get from one place to another
   b. a way that a bus or train regularly travels

4. Several countries wanted to find a northwest <u>passage</u>—a way to reach the Pacific Ocean and then Asia.
   a. a short piece of writing
   b. a way through something

5. The Corps of Discovery had 33 members. Only one person in the <u>group</u> died during the long, difficult journey.
   a. to put similar things together
   b. a number of people who are connected by an activity

© New Readers Press. All rights reserved.

Unit 1 Review

Circle the letter of the answer that best completes each sentence.

1. The **geography** of the lands that Lewis and Clark explored included _____.

   a. clouds
   b. mountains
   c. mosquitos

2. A person who is going on a **journey** is most likely going to _____.

   a. a room in his or her house
   b. a shop down the street
   c. a location across the country

3. A person will **starve** if he or she does not get enough _____.

   a. shelter
   b. food
   c. activity

4. When you **inspect** something, you _____.

   a. look at it closely
   b. guess about it
   c. ignore it

Choose the best word to finish each sentence. Write it on the line.

5. Some of the _____ taken on the expedition included 193 pounds of "portable soup," a thick paste made of beef, eggs, and vegetables.

   specimens   **provisions**   **passages**

6. Lewis and Clark were not able to find a water _____ across North America. The explorers discovered that they could not easily get from the Missouri River to a river that went to the Pacific Ocean.

   route   **region**   **problem**

7. The Louisiana Territory was _____ from France in 1803 for $15 million, or about four cents per acre of land.

   arranged   **acquired**   **appointed**

8. Lewis and Clark _____ many sewing materials, such as sewing needles, thread, and thimbles, to use as gifts for Indians.

   prohibited   **protected**   **procured**

Compared to the early 1800s, how would exploring a large region like the Louisiana Purchase be different today? Write your answer on a separate sheet of paper. Use at least five words you learned in this unit. Circle the vocabulary words you use.

© New Readers Press. All rights reserved.

TESTING TIP:

When you answer a multiple-choice vocabulary question, you select an answer from several choices. Read all of the choices before you choose one. Cross out any that you know are incorrect. If you are trying to pick a correct word meaning, try replacing the word or blank with each answer choice. Which answer makes the most sense in the sentence?

Circle the letter of the best answer.

1. **Which meaning of *territory* matches how the word is used in this sentence?**

   The Louisiana Purchase added a huge <u>territory</u> to the United States.

   A land that is part of a country but not given full rights of a state

   B an area that an animal considers its own and defends

   C an area of experience or knowledge

   D an area in a state or country that a person is responsible for as part of work

2. **What does the word *proceed* mean in this sentence?**

   Although Lewis and Clark started their trip in 1804, they could not <u>proceed</u> from Fort Mandan until the spring of 1805, when the ice thawed.

   A continue doing something

   B write down what they saw

   C keep safe from harm

   D stop something from being done

3. **Which word means "one of the large land masses on Earth"?**

   A geography

   B region

   C expedition

   D continent

4. **Which meaning of *stretched* matches how the word is used in this sentence?**

   The land that the U.S. bought from France <u>stretched</u> from the Mississippi River to the Rocky Mountains.

   A pulled to make longer

   B reached for something

   C continued over a distance

   D used something for longer time than planned

5. **Which word best completes the sentence?**

   Lewis made careful _____ about plants, such as where they grew, what they looked like, and how the Indians used them.

   A missions

   B objects

   C supplies

   D observations

6. **What word in the passage means about the same as *specimens*?**

   Lewis and Clark collected <u>specimens</u> of plants and animals that were new to science at the time. The samples were packed in the large boat along with maps and reports and sent back to St. Louis.

   A science

   B samples

   C boat

   D reports

Check your answers on page 104.

© New Readers Press. All rights reserved.

2 The Civil War

VOCABULARY

Read these words from the passage. Check the words you know.

- ☐ abolitionists
- ☐ labor
- ☐ plantations
- ☐ preserve
- ☐ secede
- ☐ slavery

Functional Vocabulary

- ☐ opposed

Slavery, Lincoln, and Emancipation

As people continued to move west across the United States in the first part of the 19th century, the country grew, new states entered the Union, and the topic of slavery divided the country.

The question was whether new states would allow **slavery**. Northerners didn't want slavery to spread west. **Abolitionists** thought slavery was wrong and wanted to end it completely. But for many years, the Southern economy had depended on growing cotton and tobacco on large **plantations** that required slave **labor**. Southerners wanted the new states to become slave states.

Although he was not an abolitionist, Abraham Lincoln **opposed** slavery. Southerners said they would **secede** from the Union if he were elected president. In the months following Lincoln's election in 1860, 11 Southern states seceded. They formed the Confederate States of America (the CSA), with Jefferson Davis as their president.

When the American Civil War began in 1861, President Lincoln wanted to **preserve** the Union, not necessarily to end slavery. In 1862, he wrote, "If I could save the Union without freeing any slave, I would do it; and if I could save it by freeing all the slaves, I would do it; and if I could save it by freeing some and leaving others alone, I would also do that." However, in 1863, he signed the Emancipation [freedom from slavery] Proclamation and freed the slaves in Confederate states. The proclamation didn't end slavery, but it made freeing slaves an important goal of the war.

1. Vocabulary Focus

Write each word from the vocabulary list beside its definition.

_____ 1. the condition of being owned by and forced to work for someone

_____ 2. people who wanted to end or stop slavery completely

_____ 3. workers

_____ 4. large areas of land where crops like sugar, cotton, and coffee are grown

_____ 5. to leave or break away

_____ 6. disagreed with something strongly

_____ 7. to keep something from harm or loss

© New Readers Press. All rights reserved.

The Battle of Gettysburg and the Gettysburg Address

The American Civil War lasted from 1861 to 1865. One of the most important fights took place between July 1 and 3, 1863. It was the **Battle** of Gettysburg.

In June of 1863, General Robert E. Lee, the leader of the Confederate Army, crossed the Southern **border** into the Northern state of Pennsylvania. His plan was to **defeat** the Union Army and continue north. Fighting began around Gettysburg on July 1 and lasted for three days. Although it was not the largest battle of the Civil War, it was the bloodiest. About 51,000 men were killed, **wounded**, taken prisoner, or listed as missing.

Gettysburg was not the end of the war, but it is often called a "turning point." Lee had hoped to force General George G. Meade, a leader of the Union Army, to **surrender**. But Lee lost the battle; he never did **invade** the North as he had wanted.

Four months later, at the **dedication** of the battlefield, President Lincoln gave the famous Gettysburg Address. Lincoln said it was everyone's responsibility to make sure that "government of the people, by the people, for the people, shall not perish [die] from the Earth." He encouraged the North to keep fighting for a united country and the end of slavery.

2. Vocabulary Focus

Complete each sentence with a word from the vocabulary list.

1. Four slave states didn't secede from the Union. They were called "_____ states" because they were on the southern edges of the Union.

2. Tens of thousands of men were killed at Gettysburg. It was a bloody _____.

3. The line of wagons filled with _____, or injured, Confederate soldiers heading South after the Battle of Gettysburg was 17 miles long.

4. Meade is best-known for his _____ of Lee at Gettysburg.

5. Gettysburg changed American history. General Lee and his army were never able to _____, or enter and occupy, the North again.

6. President Lincoln spoke at the _____ of Gettysburg, when the battlefield became an official resting place for Union dead.

7. The Civil War ended when General Lee decided to _____ and stop fighting.

VOCABULARY

Read these words from the passage. Check the words you know.

- [ ] battle
- [ ] dedication
- [ ] defeat
- [ ] invade
- [ ] surrender
- [ ] wounded

Functional Vocabulary

- [ ] border

© New Readers Press. All rights reserved.

3. Work With New Vocabulary

Answer the questions. Explain your answers.

1. Why do you think there was **slavery** in the South, but not in the North?

   _____

2. What state do you live in? What states are on its **borders**?

   _____

3. When do armies stop fighting and decide to **surrender**?

   _____

4. Authors often write a **dedication** at the beginning of a book. If you wrote a book about your life, what would the dedication say?

   _____

5. What do you imagine life was like for slave owners on a **plantation**? For the slaves?

   _____

6. Abraham Lincoln **opposed** slavery, but he was not an **abolitionist**. What is the difference between the two?

   _____

7. A war consists of many **battles**. What does it mean "to win the battle, but lose the war"?

   _____

8. What is one thing in your life today that you would like to **preserve** for the future? Why?

   _____

9. Is it ever the right thing for one state or country to **invade** another? Explain your answer.

   _____

10. What does it feel like when you **defeat** another person (or team) in sports, games, or other competition? What does it feel like when you lose?

   _____

© New Readers Press. All rights reserved.

4. Prefix uni–

The prefix *uni–* means "one." For example, police officers all wear the same uniform; they all dress in one way.

Use a word from the list to complete each sentence.

unify	union	unique	united	university

1. During the Civil War, the Northern states were also called "the _____."

2. Abraham Lincoln wanted to _____ the states and abolish slavery.

3. The Civil War was _____. For example, it was the first war to be photographed.

4. In 1865, the war ended and the states were _____ again.

5. You can learn more about the war at the Civil War Institute at American _____ in Washington, D.C., and other schools and museums around the country.

> Other "number" prefixes include *bi–* (two), *tri–* (three), and *quad–* (four).

5. Roots *cede, ceed, cess*

The roots *cede*, *ceed*, and *cess* mean "to go." These roots combine with other roots and suffixes, but not with base words that can stand alone.

Complete each sentence with a word from the list. If you aren't sure of a word's meaning, look it up in the dictionary.

access	exceeded	preceded	proceed	secede	successful

1. The National Archives gives the public _____ to multiple Civil War records.

2. The number of American lives lost in the Civil War _____ the total number lost in all wars the country had fought added together.

3. Abraham Lincoln's election _____ the Civil War.

4. Although the border states allowed slavery, they chose not to _____ from the Union.

5. After losing at Gettysburg, General Lee decided to _____ back South.

6. Lincoln was a very _____ politician and lawyer, but he also had many failures.

> The words *precede* and *proceed* sound alike and mean similar things. *Precede* means "to go before." *Proceed* means "to move ahead; to continue."

> When *Union* is capitalized, it means "the United States" (especially the Northern states during the Civil War).

© New Readers Press. All rights reserved.

6. Context Clues: General Clues and Antonyms

To determine the meaning of an unknown word, look for a context clue in the parts of the sentence that surround the word. You may also need to look at the sentences before and/or after the sentence with the new word. You can use whatever information is available to figure out the meaning.

Read the paragraphs. Look for clues to help you understand the meanings of the boldfaced words. Then complete the definitions.

Matthew Brady was a well-known 19th century photographer and one of the first to use photography to **document** national history. When the Civil War began, he organized a group of photographers to follow the **troops** into battle. He later said, "I felt that I had to go . . . and I went."

Matthew Brady and his **associates** photographed battlefields, camps, towns, and people. In 1862, Brady held an exhibition of **images** of the battlefield dead. People were stunned. A writer for *The New York Times* said that Brady brought "home to us the terrible **reality**" of war.

1. When you **document** something, you _____

2. **Troops** are _____

3. **Associates** are _____

4. **Images** are _____

5. **Reality** is _____

Words like *however, instead (of), while,* and *though* are clues that the writer is giving contrasting information.

You know you can understand the meaning of a new word by finding clues that explain the word. Antonyms are also clues; they give an opposite meaning.

Underline any examples that help explain the boldfaced words. Then write a definition for each word. Check your answers in a dictionary.

6. The Union was **industrialized** and had more cities, while the Confederacy relied mostly on farming.

   definition: _____

7. Slave-owners didn't want federal laws to **interfere** with what they thought was their business. Instead, they wanted the national government to stay out of state government.

   definition: _____

8. Abraham Lincoln gave his first **inaugural** address on March 4, 1861. He spoke as the new president of a divided country.

   definition: _____

9. Matthew Brady **chronicled** the American Civil War by telling the history of the war through photographs.

   definition: _____

7. Parts of Speech and the Dictionary

If you want to increase your vocabulary and use new words correctly, you need to know what part each word plays in speech. Some words, like *close* **and** *run,* **can be used as more than one part of speech.**

On the short line, write the part of speech of each boldfaced word. Then look up the word in a dictionary and write the definition that matches how the word is used in the sentence.

1. The Battle of Gettysburg changed the **course** of the Civil War.

   _____ _____

2. Before Gettysburg, the Union had experienced a **string** of losses.

   _____ _____

3. Abraham Lincoln was opposed to the **spread** of slavery.

   _____ _____

4. He used the dedication of Gettysburg's Soldiers National Cemetery to **honor** the Union dead.

   _____ _____

5. He said, "We have come to dedicate a portion of that field as a final resting place for those who here gave their lives . . . It is altogether **fitting** and proper that we should do this."

   _____ _____

> If the word *a, an,* or *the* comes right before a word, the word is not a verb. For example, *document* is a noun in this sentence: *The document is in the National Civil War Museum.*

8. Multiple-Meaning Words

A word can have multiple meanings within one part of speech. For example, *cross* **can be a verb or a noun. But both the noun and the verb have multiple meanings.**

Look at the underlined word. Circle the letter of the best definition.

1. For years before the Civil War began, groups such as abolitionists had tried to <u>reform</u> America by calling for an end to slavery as well as equal rights for women and aid for the poor.
   a. to improve something by changing it
   b. to correct a person's behavior or habits

2. On the third day of the Battle of Gettysburg, General Lee sent 12,500 of his troops to <u>charge</u> General Meade's army.
   a. move forward to quickly; rush into
   b. buy something and agree to pay for it later

3. President Lincoln's <u>address</u> at Gettysburg took less than three minutes.
   a. the place where a person can usually be reached
   b. a formal speech

4. In it, he said, "The world will little <u>note</u>, nor long remember, what we say here, but it can never forget what they [the dead] did here." Would he be surprised to know that the Gettysburg Address is one of the most famous speeches in history?
   a. notice or pay attention to something
   b. record something in writing

© New Readers Press. All rights reserved.

Unit 2 Review

Write the pair of words that best completes each sentence.

1. _____ in the North _____ slavery.

    Abolitionists   **Associates**   **opposed**   **preserved**

2. Lincoln wanted to _____ the Union, but the Southern states

   _____ anyway.

    invade   **preserve**   **interfered**   **seceded**

3. Although many _____ were lost at the Battle of Gettysburg, the South did not

   _____ for another two years.

    associates   **troops**   **spread**   **surrender**

4. Large plantations required slave _____ that the more _____ North did not.

    images   **labor**   **industrialized**   **unique**

Circle the letter of the answer that best completes each sentence.

5. When Confederate troops **invaded** Pennsylvania in 1863, they _____.

   a. crossed the border
   b. unified the country
   c. spread slavery

6. Battles that **preceded** Gettysburg _____.

   a. interfered with Gettysburg
   b. took place before Gettysburg
   c. honored Gettysburg

7. When you look at Matthew Brady's **images**, you see _____ showing the reality of war.

   a. borders
   b. photos
   c. plantations

8. If a vote is **unanimous**, _____.

   a. everyone voted for the same person
   b. one person voted
   c. all the votes add up to 100 percent

Why do you think many Americans find the Civil War so interesting? Write your answer on a separate sheet of paper. Use at least five words you learned in this unit. Circle the vocabulary words you use.

© New Readers Press. All rights reserved.

TESTING TIP:

When you're taking a test with multiple-choice questions, try to come up with the answer in your head before you read the options.

Circle the letter of the best answer.

1. **What is the meaning of *course* in this passage?**

   The Battle of Gettysburg took place between July 1 and July 3, 1863. More than 30,000 men were wounded over the <u>course</u> of those three days.

   A a part of a meal served separately

   B a set of university classes on one subject

   C the way something progresses or develops

   D the path something takes as it moves

2. **Which word best completes the passage?**

   The Confederate States _____ from the Union shortly after Lincoln became president in 1860. The Civil War started not long after that in 1861.

   A defeated

   B invaded

   C seceded

   D interfered

3. **Which words best describe something that is *unique*?**

   A one of a kind

   B of one opinion

   C made into one

   D one sided

4. **Which word from the passage means about the same as *address*?**

   A photo of Lincoln taken during his inaugural <u>address</u> in 1861 shows him giving his first speech as president. Even then, it was an accepted reality that the South would soon secede from the Union.

   A image

   B speech

   C president

   D reality

5. **Which word best completes the sentence?**

   The troops _____ in a straight line.

   A exceeded

   B preceded

   C proceeded

   D seceded

6. **What kind of people are you most likely to find in a hospital?**

   A wounded

   B honored

   C associates

   D reformed

Check your answers on page 104.

© New Readers Press. All rights reserved.

3 Immigration

VOCABULARY

Read these words from the passage. Check the words you know.

- ☐ citizen
- ☐ famine
- ☐ freedom
- ☐ immigration
- ☐ persecution
- ☐ settle

Functional Vocabulary

- ☐ majority

A Nation of Immigrants

All Americans except Native Americans have a family history of **immigration**. Most immigrants came here by choice, hoping to experience the American dream—the belief that anyone who tries hard enough can succeed.

In 1790, the U.S. Congress passed the first Naturalization Act, which stated that anyone "being a free white person" may become a **citizen** of the United States. For the next 100 years, Congress didn't do much about immigration. It was the responsibility of the individual states.

Between 1815 and 1865, millions of immigrants moved to the United States looking for **freedom** from **persecution** and for an opportunity to improve their lives. The **majority** of these "old immigrants" were from northern and western Europe. For example, over 4.5 million of them came from Ireland, which experienced a terrible potato **famine** in the mid-19th century. Another 2 million immigrants came to the United States to leave behind political changes and economic problems in Germany.

At the same time, the United States was expanding to the west. The Industrial Revolution was beginning, gold had been discovered in California, and slavery was coming to an end. Millions of European and Asian immigrants entered the United States to **settle** in the Midwest and on the West Coast. There was room for everyone.

1. Vocabulary Focus

Write each word from the vocabulary list beside its definition.

_____ 1. the process of moving to a new country to stay

_____ 2. a member of a state

_____ 3. a period when there is not enough food for many people for a long time

_____ 4. move to a place and make it your home

_____ 5. the greater number

_____ 6. the right not to be subject to something bad

_____ 7. being treated in a mean and harmful way because of differences in race, religion, point of view, etc.

© New Readers Press. All rights reserved.

1880 to 1920 and the New Immigrants

The Immigration Act of 1891 gave responsibility for immigration to the federal government. The U.S. opened Ellis Island in New York harbor as a federal immigration station in 1892.

From 1880 to 1920, more than 20 million immigrants arrived in the United States. Most of these "new immigrants" came from central, eastern, and southern Europe. They left their homes, friends, and families; they also left behind disease, poverty, war, and religious persecution.

During the early 1900s, Ellis Island was the main **port** of arrival for European immigrants. Over the 62 years it served as the entry point, more than 12 million people entered the U.S. through Ellis Island. Most immigrants spent only a few hours on the island, but those with medical or **legal** problems were **detained** longer. Only about two percent of them were sent back to their old countries, usually because they failed medical or government **inspections**.

Not all new immigrants were welcomed—some experienced **prejudice** from native-born Americans and other immigrant groups. These anti-immigrant feelings increased after the U.S. entered World War I in 1917. Although immigration began to **rise** again after the war, new federal laws **limited** the number and nationalities of immigrants allowed into the country.

2. Vocabulary Focus

Write the word from the vocabulary list that best matches the underlined word or words.

_____ 1. Some immigrants who left their old countries because of <u>unfair treatment based on race, politics, religion, etc.</u> faced similar problems in the United States.

_____ 2. During <u>acts of getting information</u>, immigrants met doctors and government officials.

_____ 3. On Ellis Island, immigrants discussed <u>related-to-the-law</u> problems with government officials and lawyers.

_____ 4. In 1910, Angel Island opened in California as a <u>place where people and goods can enter a country</u> of entry on the West Coast.

_____ 5. In general, immigrants who arrived at Angel Island were <u>legally prevented from leaving</u> longer than immigrants at Ellis Island.

_____ 6. The large number of people crowding into cities caused feelings against immigrants to <u>increase</u>.

_____ 7. The Immigration Act of 1924 <u>reduced</u> the number of immigrants allowed into the United States.

© New Readers Press. All rights reserved.

VOCABULARY

Read these words from the passage. Check the words you know.

- [ ] detained
- [ ] inspections
- [ ] legal
- [ ] limited
- [ ] port
- [ ] prejudice

Functional Vocabulary

- [ ] rise

3. Work With New Vocabulary

Answer the questions. Explain your answers.

1. What is the importance of **immigration** in the history of the United States?

   _____

2. What are some reasons people today give for feeling **prejudiced** against people they've never met?

   _____

3. What does it mean to you to be a good **citizen**?

   _____

4. Although there were many **ports** of entry for immigrants, the largest ports were on the East Coast. Why do you think this was the case?

   _____

5. Immigrant-aid societies helped immigrants **settle** in the United States. What kinds of services do you think they provided?

   _____

Rise can also be a verb meaning "get/go up" or "increase." For example, you know that the Sun will rise every morning.

6. Why do you think a war would cause a **rise** in anti-immigration feelings?

   _____

7. Name two things you have the **freedom** to do because you live in the United States. Would you leave if you couldn't do those things? Why or why not?

   _____

8. Why do you think people in the United States still want to **limit** the rights of immigrants today?

   _____

9. What was the purpose of medical **inspections** at immigration stations? Were they necessary?

   _____

10. Where did the **majority** of your family emigrate from? When did they come to the United States?

    _____

11. How do you think immigrants and their families felt when they were **detained** at Ellis Island? What do you think they did during that time?

    _____

© New Readers Press. All rights reserved.

4. Prefix *anti–*

The prefix *anti–* means "against" or "opposite of," so it is called a "negative prefix." The prefix *anti–* is often added to adjectives (*antibiotic*) and nouns (*antihero*).

Complete each sentence with a word from the list.

anti-democratic	anti-immigrant	antislavery	antisocial	antiwar

1. Many creative people prefer to be alone. Are they _____ because they don't enjoy spending time with other people?

2. Thomas Jefferson, the third president of the United States, was opposed to slavery. He said it was _____ and a threat to the nation. However, Jefferson owned slaves.

3. Preceding the Civil War, abolitionists in the Northern states were _____. They wanted everyone in every state to be free.

4. In the 1960s, _____ protestors marched in Washington, D.C., and other U.S. cities against the fighting in Vietnam.

5. People who are _____ don't want any more newcomers to enter the United States.

> It is easy to confuse the prefix *anti–* with the prefix *ante–* (meaning "before").

5. Root *migr*

The root *migr* means "move." Read the definitions of these words with the root *migr*.

    emigrants: people who leave a country to move to a new one
    emigrate: to leave a country to move to a new one
    migrants: people who move from place to place
    migrate: to move from one place to another, often temporarily
    migration: the process of moving from one place to another
    migratory: regularly moving to another place

Choose a word from the list to complete each sentence. If you aren't sure of a word's meaning, look it up in the dictionary.

1. Before World War I, many _____ left Europe to keep their families safe.

2. Millions of workers who pick fruit, vegetables, and nuts in the United States are _____ and move from one farm to another in order to find work.

3. Gray whales _____ about 10,000 miles between Mexico and the Arctic every year.

4. Arnold Schwarzeneger decided to _____ from Austria when he was 21 years old.

5. Because of the Great Depression and the Dust Bowl, there was a large _____ of Americans from the Midwest to the West during the 1930s.

6. Snow geese are _____ birds. Every year, they fly south for the winter in order to find food.

> Animals, plants, ideas, etc. can migrate, too.

© New Readers Press. All rights reserved.

6. Context Clues: General Clues and Definitions

When you're trying to figure out the meaning of a new word, look at the words that come before and after it. Those words may help you with the meaning and structure of the new word and will show how it is used.

Read the paragraph. Look for clues to help you understand the meanings of the boldfaced words. Then complete the definitions of those words.

The Ellis Island Immigration Station opened on January 1, 1892. Annie Moore, a teenaged girl from County Cork, Ireland, was the first immigrant **admitted** to Ellis Island. **Approximately** 700 immigrants arrived that same day; the number isn't exact. Annie and her two younger brothers made the 12-day **journey** across the Atlantic Ocean on their own. Later, she and her brothers were **reunited** with their parents, who were already living in New York.

1. A _____ is a long trip from one place to another.

2. _____ means "not exactly, roughly."

3. People are _____ when they come together again after a long period of time.

4. When you are _____ somewhere, you are allowed to enter.

Sometimes you can understand the meaning of an unfamiliar word by finding words or clues that are examples of the word.

Underline any examples that help explain the boldfaced words. Then write a definition for each word. Check your answers in a dictionary.

5. It is estimated that 40 percent of all Americans have at least one **ancestor** who came through Ellis Island. People can go online to find out how their family members from the past arrived in the United States.

   definition: _____

6. The Moore children traveled on the SS Nevada in **steerage**, the cheapest and most crowded level on the ship.

   definition: _____

SS is the abbreviation for steamship.

7. Families from Ireland, Russia, and Austria, who came to the United States through Ellis Island, added to the cultural **diversity** of the United States.

   definition: _____

8. Today, Ellis Island is one of the most popular tourist **destinations** in the National Park Service. It's such an interesting place that I'm not surprised people like to go there.

   definition: _____

© New Readers Press. All rights reserved.

7. Parts of Speech and the Dictionary

Understanding the parts of speech and how they fit together makes writing and reading easier. All words are assigned to a part of speech according to the part they play in a sentence.

On the short line, write the part of speech of each boldfaced word. Then look up the word in a dictionary and write the definition that matches how the word is used in the sentence.

1. There have been four major **waves** of immigration in U.S. history.

   _____ _____

2. In the 1840s, the Irish potato famine played a key role in **mass** immigration to the United States.

   _____ _____

3. Between 1880 and 1920, the majority of European emigrants to the United States **landed** on Ellis Island.

   _____ _____

4. Because of anti-immigrant feelings, Congress began to **pass** laws that limited immigration.

   _____ _____

5. In the early part of the 19th century, immigration to the United States was **light**—about 6,000 people a year.

   _____ _____

8. Multiple-Meaning Words

To determine which is the best definition, first read the sentence. Then reread it, replacing the underlined word with answer option *a*. Reread it again, this time inserting answer option *b*. Ask yourself which of the new sentences matches the meaning of the original most closely.

Look at each underlined word. Circle the letter of the best definition.

1. Before 1965, immigration laws were written to <u>favor</u> Europeans. Today, the majority of immigrants to the United States come from Asia and Latin America.
   a. show approval of
   b. treat someone better than someone else, in an unfair way

2. The first immigration station on Ellis Island burned down in 1897. Important <u>records</u> that went back to 1855 were lost.
   a. thin plastic disks carrying music
   b. historic information which is kept in files on paper or stored electronically

3. Hundreds of thousands of people from southern and eastern Europe <u>flooded</u> the United States in the early 1920s.
   a. covered a place or area with water
   b. arrived in large amounts or numbers

4. Bad times and poor conditions in Europe <u>drove</u> people out, while land, freedom, and opportunity in the United States pulled them in.
   a. traveled by car
   b. caused to go

- Both of the answer options in the question are definitions of the underlined word.

- When the word *records* is a noun, the stress is on the first syllable. When *records* is a verb, the stress is on the second syllable.

© New Readers Press. All rights reserved.

Unit 3 Review

Circle the letter of the answer that best completes each sentence.

1. People who faced **persecution** in their homelands immigrated to the United States to seek _____.

    a. prejudice

    b. famine

    c. freedom

2. A neighborhood that has a lot of cultural **diversity** probably has people _____.

    a. from many countries

    b. from Ireland

    c. who are antisocial

3. Immigrants who were _____ were often **detained** at Ellis Island.

    a. sick

    b. hungry

    c. citizens

4. If opportunities are **limited**, there are _____ chances to succeed.

    a. many

    b. few

    c. no

Choose the best word to finish each sentence. Write it on the line.

5. Many immigrants were _____ with their families after being apart for many years.

    reunited   **admitted**   **landed**

6. You can research your _____ by checking records at the U.S. Citizenship and Immigration Services.

    citizens   **ancestors**   **emigrants**

7. It took an average of seven hours to _____ through Ellis Island.

    pass   **flood**   **settle**

8. New York was not always the final _____ for people who landed at Ellis Island. Many took trains to other cities or states.

    port   **destination**   **journey**

Why do you think some immigrants called Ellis Island "the Island of Hope," and others called it "the Island of Tears"? Write your answer on a separate sheet of paper. Use at least five words you learned in this unit. Circle the vocabulary words you use.

© New Readers Press. All rights reserved.

TESTING TIP:

If you have time left when you finish a test, review your work. First, make sure you answered all the questions. Then check your answers. Change an answer only if you misread or misunderstood the question. Your first answer is usually correct.

Circle the letter of the best answer.

1. **Which choice best completes the sentence?**

   Immigrants from all over the world add to the _____ of the United States.

   A majority

   B freedom

   C diversity

   D waves

2. **Which definition of *admitted* matches how the word is used in this sentence?**

   Between 1900 and 1915, more than 15 million immigrants were <u>admitted</u> to the United States. That was about as many as arrived in the previous 40 years combined.

   A accepted as patients in a hospital

   B agreed unwillingly that something is true

   C said you have done something wrong

   D allowed to enter a place

3. **Which of the following words means "movement from one place to another"?**

   A migrate

   B migratory

   C migration

   D migrant

4. **Which choice best completes the sentence?**

   Someone who is antislavery _____.

   A thinks it's wrong to own slaves

   B believes slavery is a good idea

   C was a slave in the past

   D owns some slaves

5. **Who was most likely to travel *in steerage*?**

   A someone who had little money to spend

   B someone who had a lot of cars

   C someone who had family living in the United States

   D someone who had a lot of time to travel

6. **Which word or words from the passage mean about the same as *journeys*?**

   Immigrants made long <u>journeys</u> to ports of entry around the United States to leave behind famine, persecution, war, and economic depression. Their trips were difficult, but belief in the American dream made it a little easier for them.

   A ports

   B trips

   C belief

   D dream

Check your answers beginning on page 104.

© New Readers Press. All rights reserved.

4 The 19th Amendment

VOCABULARY

Read these words from the passage. Check the words you know.

- ☐ amendment
- ☐ convention
- ☐ guaranteed
- ☐ proposed
- ☐ ratified
- ☐ suffrage

Functional Vocabulary

- ☐ extended

Women's Suffrage

The right of citizens to vote shall not be abridged [limited] by the United States or by any State on account of [based on] sex. —The 19th **Amendment** to the U.S. Constitution

In the early 19th century, women couldn't own property, sign contracts, or vote. There were many men and women who believed that women didn't need to do these things. To them, a woman's job was to get married, have children, and guide her family.

Over time, women began to push for their rights. In July 1848, Elizabeth Cady Stanton and Lucretia Mott organized the Seneca Falls **Convention**, the first women's rights convention. They argued for women's **suffrage** as a way to improve the country. They believed that American women should have the right to vote.

The 14th Amendment passed in 1868. It **guaranteed** civil rights and equal protection under the law to all citizens, but it didn't give women the right to vote. The 15th Amendment, which passed in 1870, **extended** the right to vote to black men, but not to women.

In 1878, a constitutional amendment that later became the 19th Amendment was **proposed** in Congress. The amendment didn't pass, but it was re-introduced to Congress in each of the next 41 years. Finally, on August 26, 1920, the 19th Amendment to the Constitution was **ratified**. Millions of women got the vote and continued their movement toward equality with men.

1. Vocabulary Focus

Read each sentence. Write the word from the vocabulary list that means the same thing as the underlined word or words.

_____ 1. The 19th Amendment <u>made available</u> the right to vote to women.

_____ 2. The Bill of Rights <u>formally promised</u> the right to free speech.

_____ 3. In his speech, the mayor <u>suggested</u> cutting the city's taxes.

_____ 4. In 1920, a <u>change</u> to the U.S. Constitution gave women the right to vote.

_____ 5. Several European countries did not extend <u>voting rights</u> to women until the 1940s.

_____ 6. Do you know when the governors' <u>large meeting</u> is?

_____ 7. The 13th Amendment, which ended slavery in the U.S., was <u>formally approved</u> in 1865.

© New Readers Press. All rights reserved.

Protests During the Suffrage Movement

In the first part of the 20th Century, some suffragists participated in public protests and **demonstrations** to gain attention for their cause.

Suffrage groups across the country didn't always agree on the best ways to bring about **reform**. Some leaders believed that powerful public actions were necessary. Alice Paul and Lucy Burns **organized** public parades and large meetings. At the time, "respectable" women just didn't go walking alone, so many people were shocked by the suffragists' behavior. As a result, the suffrage **movement** got additional attention.

In 1913, one group of suffragists held a national demonstration in Washington, D.C. About 8,000 women marched in front of 500,000 people. Things became violent. Some men, including police officers, attacked the marchers. Newspapers printed disturbing photographs of men dragging women through the streets. These pictures helped bring the **debate** on female suffrage to the attention of the U.S. Congress.

Suffragists used many forms of **civil disobedience** to get their voices heard. Some women **protested** for the right to vote. They marched, gave speeches, and picketed, or carried signs and banners, in front of the White House. Many of them were arrested and sent to jail. While they were in jail, some of the protestors went on hunger strikes. Some were beaten. But women continued to demonstrate and organize meetings. In the end, they built the support they needed to get the 19th Amendment passed.

VOCABULARY

Read these words from the passage. Check the words you know.

- [ ] civil disobedience
- [ ] debate
- [ ] demonstrations
- [ ] movement
- [ ] protested
- [ ] reform

Functional Vocabulary

- [ ] organized

2. Vocabulary Focus

Write each word from the vocabulary list beside its definition:

_____ 1. events in which groups of people show that they support or oppose someone or something

_____ 2. a positive change

_____ 3. active refusal to obey certain laws, demands, or commands of government, usually using peaceful methods

_____ 4. gathered people into a group to do something together

_____ 5. a series of activities in which many people work together to achieve a goal

_____ 6. publicly showed strong disapproval or support of something

_____ 7. a discussion in which people express their opinions

© New Readers Press. All rights reserved.

3. Work With New Vocabulary

Answer the questions. Explain your answers.

1. Why would a national **convention** most likely be held in a city with a lot of hotels?

   _____

2. If you could propose an **amendment** to the Constitution, what would it be?

   _____

3. What are some actions that are examples of **civil disobedience**?

   _____

> Words that end with *–ize* are verbs. Do you know the meanings of these *–ize* verbs?
>
> *organize*
> *legalize*
> *socialize*
> *realize*
> *theorize*

4. Would it be easier to **organize** a large public meeting for women's suffrage today than it was in the early 1900s? Explain your answer.

   _____

5. Why do you think it took so many years for the 19th Amendment to be **ratified**?

   _____

6. What would make you decide to join a social **movement**?

   _____

7. The hospital workers stood in front of city hall and held signs saying, "More patients? More rooms!" Is that an example of a **demonstration**? Explain.

   _____

8. What can U.S. citizens do to push for **reform** in government?

   _____

9. What is something that students might **protest** about at school?

   _____

10. Why do you think people participate in public **debates** on TV?

    _____

11. Does the U.S. Constitution **guarantee** all U.S. citizens the same rights? Explain.

    _____

12. Do you think everyone was happy when voting rights were **extended** to women? Explain.

    _____

© New Readers Press. All rights reserved.

4. Roots *mand*, *mend*

The roots *mand* and *mend* mean "to order or command." You can combine these roots with other word parts to form new words, such as *command* or *recommendation*.

Choose a word from the list to complete each sentence. If you aren't sure of a word's meaning, look it up in the dictionary.

When you read an unfamiliar word, see if you can find a shorter word or a word part that you know inside the longer word.

amended	commander	demands	mandatory	recommend	reprimanded

1. The president of the United States is the _____-in-chief of the nation's military.

2. One part of the U.S. Constitution describes how the Constitution can be _____.

3. Most people don't enjoy paying income tax, but taxes are _____ in this country.

4. The protesters had a list of _____ for the mayor.

5. The general _____ the soldier for not listening to his orders.

6. Ms. Stewart thinks highly of Tom. She will _____ him for the job.

5. Suffixes *–ion*, *–tion*, *–ation*

When the suffix *–ion*, *–tion*, or *–ation* is added to a verb, it turns the verb into a noun. These suffixes mean "the act or process of doing something." For example, the verb *create* + the suffix *–ion* = the noun *creation*, which means "the act or process of creating something or making something new."

Add the suffix –ion, –tion, or –ation to each verb to make a noun. Write the noun on the line.

1. migrate _____

2. organize _____

3. protect _____

4. separate _____

5. demonstrate _____

6. introduce _____

The underlined word in each sentence has the suffix –ion or –tion. Write the definition of the underlined word. Use a dictionary to check your answers.

7. The crowds had mixed <u>reactions</u> when they watched the suffrage parades.

    definition: _____

8. The expert's <u>prediction</u> about who would become president was incorrect.

    definition: _____

9. An <u>election</u> for president of the United States is held every four years in November.

    definition: _____

© New Readers Press. All rights reserved.

6. Context Clues: General Clues, Definitions, and Examples

If you're trying to figure out the meaning of an unfamiliar word, look for a definition or for clues in what comes before and after the word.

Read the paragraph. Look for clues to help you understand the meaning of each boldfaced word. Write the meaning on the line.

The state of Tennessee provided the votes necessary to ratify the 19th Amendment. Harry T. Burn, a Tennessee **legislator**, had previously been **opposed** to suffrage, but he changed his mind and voted for it. His mother had written him a letter that **advised** him to "be a good boy" and vote for suffrage. Burn explained, "I know a mother's advice is always safest for her boy to follow, and my mother wanted me to vote for ratification." He said that it was the **moral** choice to ratify, that his decision to change his vote was based on doing the right and good thing.

The words *advise* and *advice* are often confused. *Advise* is a verb, while *advice* is a noun.

1. A **legislator** is _____

2. To be **opposed** to something means to be _____

3. To **advise** means to _____

4. **Moral** means _____

Sometimes you can understand the meaning of an unfamiliar word by finding words or clues that are examples of the word.

Underline any examples that help explain the boldfaced words. Then write a definition for each word. Check your answers in a dictionary.

The words *for example*, *such as*, *including*, and *for instance* are clues that a writer is giving examples.

5. In the early 19th century, laws in most states didn't allow a woman to own or **inherit** property. For example, if her father died, her brother would receive all of his money.

   definition: _____

6. The **sacrifices** made by women during World War I, such as losing their loved ones and leaving their homes to work at dangerous jobs, were one reason the 19th Amendment was finally passed.

   definition: _____

7. Suffragists **advocated** for the right to vote by arguing, debating, sharing stories, writing letters, and more.

   definition: _____

8. On November 2, 1920, an **estimated** eight million women voted in elections for the first time; the exact number is unknown.

   definition: _____

© New Readers Press. All rights reserved.

7. Parts of Speech and the Dictionary

Some words can play more than one part in speech. For example, the word *state* **can be a noun meaning "a part of a country."** *State* **can also be a verb meaning "to write or say something." When you look up a word in the dictionary, check that the part of speech and the meaning match the use you are checking.**

Look at each boldfaced word. What part of speech does it play? Circle noun *or* verb. *Then look up the word in a dictionary. Write the correct definition on the line.*

noun   verb   1. Some leaders did not **support** the suffrage movement.

_____

noun   verb   2. The government cannot **force** U.S. citizens to vote.

_____

noun   verb   3. Did you **notice** the small group of protesters outside City Hall?

_____

noun   verb   4. There is no **guarantee** that the government will pass the bill this year.

_____

noun   verb   5. The company signed a **contract** that said the work would be done on time.

_____

8. Multiple-Meaning Words

Some words have more than one meaning. To figure out the correct meaning, look at how the word is used in the sentence. You can also look at nearby words and sentences for clues.

Look at each underlined word. Circle the letter of the best definition.

1. The 22nd Amendment limits the number of <u>terms</u> a president can serve.
   a. words or phrases that name something
   b. periods of time that something lasts

2. President Woodrow Wilson was in <u>office</u> when the 19th Amendment passed.
   a. a position in government
   b. a room where people work

3. In the early 1800s, many states did not allow married women to buy or sell <u>property</u>.
   a. a characteristic or quality of something
   b. things that someone owns

4. Suffragists were the first people to <u>picket</u> in front of the White House.
   a. stand outside and protest
   b. a piece of wood in a fence

> Think about how a word is used. Choose an answer that matches the part of speech.

© New Readers Press. All rights reserved.

Unit 4 Review

Circle the letter of the answer that best completes each sentence.

1. If you are a **legislator**, you have the power to _____.
   a. lead armies
   b. make laws
   c. force people to vote

2. If something is **mandatory**, it is something that you _____.
   a. refuse to do
   b. hate to do
   c. must do

3. People try to pass **amendments** to the U.S. Constitution because they _____.
   a. want to change it
   b. think it should be longer
   c. want to get rid of it

4. People would be most likely to **protest** in public about _____.
   a. a bad movie
   b. an unfair law
   c. the food in a restaurant

Choose the best word to finish each sentence. Write it on the line.

5. Women used acts of _____, such as parades and marches, to get the right to vote.

   guarantees   **civil disobedience**   **suffrage**

6. The first women's rights _____ was held in Seneca Falls, New York, in 1848.

   commander   **contract**   **convention**

7. The 19th Amendment, which gave women the right to vote, was _____, or passed, in 1920.

   ratified   **guaranteed**   **protested**

8. At a political _____, the candidates [people who want to be elected] argue their views on important issues.

   movement   **debate**   **contract**

Why do you think it was important for different groups in the United States to try to get voting rights? Write your answer on a separate sheet of paper. Use at least five words you learned in this unit. Circle the vocabulary words you use.

© New Readers Press. All rights reserved.

TESTING TIP:

Some test questions will ask you to choose the correct definition of a word or term as it is used in a sentence or passage. Read the answer choices. Cross out any choices that do not apply. Then try each remaining choice in the sentence. Does it make sense? Pick the one that works best.

Circle the letter of the best answer.

1. **Which definition of *movement* matches the meaning in this passage?**

   The women's rights <u>movement</u> did not end in 1920 when women got the right to vote. There are still debates today about issues such as equal pay for women.

   A a change in an amount, such as a price

   B one section of a piece of music

   C a group of people who work together to reach shared political or social goals

   D an act of moving from one place to another

2. **What does the word *demonstration* mean in this sentence?**

   At the <u>demonstration</u>, women marched and carried signs and banners.

   A an act of showing how something is done

   B a public meeting or protest

   C a show of feelings or emotions

   D a sign displaying a political message

3. **Which of the following words means "the act or process of organizing"?**

   A organization

   B disorganized

   C reorganize

   D organizer

4. **Which words in the passage mean about the same as *suffrage*?**

   The 15th Amendment gave <u>suffrage</u> to African American men. However, in the late 1800s, their right to vote was limited by requiring them to pay poll taxes.

   A was limited

   B African American men

   C right to vote

   D requiring them to pay poll taxes

5. **Which of the following people gives orders?**

   A a legislator

   B a suffragist

   C a protester

   D a commander

6. **What is the meaning of *guarantees* as it is used in this sentence?**

   The First Amendment <u>guarantees</u> the right to free speech.

   A agreements to replace an item that breaks

   B written promises to repay money you owe

   C officially promises something

   D makes it certain something will happen

Check your answers on page 105.

© New Readers Press. All rights reserved.

5 The Great Depression

VOCABULARY

Read these words from the passage. Check the words you know.

- ☐ consumers
- ☐ depression
- ☐ economy
- ☐ income
- ☐ prosperity
- ☐ unemployment

Functional Vocabulary

- ☐ effects

The Great Depression

We shall not repeat the excesses of the wild twenties when this Nation went for a joy ride on a roller coaster which ended in a tragic crash. —President Franklin D. Roosevelt

The 1920s was a time of **prosperity** in the United States. Companies were busy making new products like radios, refrigerators, and cars, and **consumers** were busy buying them. Stock prices increased, and people made more money than ever before.

By the summer of 1929, however, the U.S. **economy** began to weaken. Then, in October 1929, the stock market crashed. It dropped 23% in one day and kept falling. The Great **Depression** had begun. Although the depression started in the United States, it spread around the world. It lasted for 10 years and changed the relationship between the U.S. government and citizens.

The **effects** of the depression were immediate and severe. People rushed to get their money out of banks. Others lost their life savings when banks failed. Worried about the future, people stopped spending. As a result, industries stopped making goods. Many businesses closed. The **unemployment** rate soared to 25 percent. Some people with jobs were paid less than before. From 1929 to 1933, family **income** dropped by 40 percent.

Hungry people waited in long lines for free soup and bread. Others became homeless. Some lived in cardboard shacks and camps called "Hoovervilles," named after President Herbert Hoover, whom many blamed for the depression.

1. Vocabulary Focus

Write each word from the vocabulary list beside its definition.

_____ 1. the state of being successful and having money

_____ 2. people who buy products and services

_____ 3. results; the way a person or event changes something

_____ 4. the state of wanting a job but not having one

_____ 5. the amount of money that a person or group makes

_____ 6. a country's system of making, selling, and buying goods and services

_____ 7. a time of low economic activity when high numbers of people have no jobs

© New Readers Press. All rights reserved.

The New Deal

President Franklin D. Roosevelt had a plan for ending the Great Depression. He called it the New Deal.

Many people blamed President Herbert Hoover for the Great Depression. They felt that Hoover did not treat the **crisis** seriously enough. Hoover didn't think the government should give **relief** to people who became jobless, homeless, and poor during the depression. In 1932, Franklin D. Roosevelt ran for president. He promised a "new deal" for the American people. Roosevelt won easily.

In Roosevelt's first 100 days in office, he put many **policies** into place. New laws helped banks stay open. People's bank deposits were protected. Creating jobs was another step in economic **recovery**. Roosevelt started the largest public works program in the country's history. People got jobs building dams and roads, planting trees, and making trails and campgrounds. The New Deal also gave aid to farmers, who suffered badly during the depression. Many farmers had a lot of **debt**, so one program gave them low-interest loans. Another program paid farmers to cut **production** of crops, which pushed crop values higher.

The best-known of Roosevelt's programs may have been the Social Security Act, passed in 1935. The Social Security Act was an old-age insurance system. It gave older Americans monthly income. Companies and workers contributed money from each paycheck to pay for those who retired. Later the program **expanded**. It covered disabled people who could not work and offered other benefits. The program still exists today.

VOCABULARY

Read these words from the passage. Check the words you know.

- ☐ crisis
- ☐ debt
- ☐ policies
- ☐ production
- ☐ recovery
- ☐ relief

Functional Vocabulary

- ☐ expanded

2. Vocabulary Focus

Complete each sentence with a word from the vocabulary list.

1. If something _____, it got bigger.

2. A _____ is a time of great difficulty or danger.

3. _____ is the process of growing or making something that can be sold.

4. _____ is when something returns to normal after a difficult time.

5. An amount of money that you owe is a _____.

6. High-level overall plans about what should be done are _____.

7. Food and money are examples of _____ given to help people.

© New Readers Press. All rights reserved.

3. Work With New Vocabulary

Read each sentence. Write T *if the statement is true. Write* F *if the statement is false and explain why it is false.*

1. _____ During a time of **prosperity**, many people do not have food, homes, jobs, or money.

   _____

2. _____ Some ways a government can give **relief** are by providing money, food, and jobs.

   _____

The word *unemployment* is a noun that can't be counted with numbers. You don't use the word *an* before *unemployment*, and it takes a singular verb. For example: *Unemployment is a serious problem in Greece.*

3. _____ During a time of high **unemployment**, almost everyone has a job.

   _____

4. _____ **Consumers** are people who make goods or offer services.

   _____

5. _____ In a **depression**, most people have jobs and a lot of money to spend.

   _____

6. _____ When something is **expanded**, it gets smaller.

   _____

7. _____ A person or country that has a lot of **debt** owes a lot of money to others.

   _____

8. _____ A country's **economy** includes the **production** and sale of goods and services.

   _____

Answer the questions. Explain your answers.

The words *effect* and *affect* are often confused. Usually *effect* is a noun that means "result," and *affect* is a verb, meaning "to produce a change in someone or something."

9. What are some **effects** when people in a country don't have enough **income**?

   _____

10. Why might creating jobs help economic **recovery**?

    _____

11. Is a **crisis** a good thing or a bad thing? Explain your answer.

    _____

12. What are some **policies** at your school or job?

    _____

© New Readers Press. All rights reserved.

4. Root *press*

The root *press* can mean "to force, squeeze, press." This root can appear at the beginning, middle, or end of a word, as in *pressure*, *compression*, *oppress*.

Match each word to its definition. Write the letter of the correct definition on the line.

_____ 1. pressure   a. to press something into a smaller space

_____ 2. oppression   b. use of fear or influence to get someone to do something

_____ 3. repress   c. to push or press down on something

_____ 4. express   d. unfair treatment of people to limit their rights

_____ 5. compress   e. to show or tell what you think or feel

_____ 6. depress   f. to use force to control people and limit their freedom

Some words with the root *press* have scientific meanings. For example, the word *depression* can mean a time of low economic activity, a mental state of sadness, or a weather condition that often causes rain. Context can help you choose the correct meaning.

5. Suffix *–ment*

The suffix *–ment* can mean "action; process" or "the result of an action." Most words that end with *–ment* are nouns. For example, when you *pay*, you give someone money for something. A *payment* is the act or process of paying for something.

Choose a word from the list to complete each sentence. If you aren't sure of a word's meaning, look it up in the dictionary.

achievement	environment	government	investments	unemployment

1. Some banks made bad _____, and they lost a lot of money.

2. During the Great Depression, many people lost their jobs, and the _____ rate grew to 25%.

3. Building the Hoover Dam was a great _____ during the 1930s.

4. Poor farming methods damaged the _____ and contributed to big dust storms in the American Midwest.

5. The federal _____ became more involved in managing the economy during the Great Depression.

The suffix *–ment* is usually added to verbs. For example, *settle + ment = settlement*.

Add the suffix –ment to each word below. Then write a definition of the new word.

6. develop: _____   _____

7. improve: _____   _____

© New Readers Press. All rights reserved.

6. Context Clues: Restatements and General Clues

Phrases like *this means, that is, also called,* and *in other words* can signal that the writer is restating an idea. A writer may also use punctuation like commas and dashes when restating something.

You can look for clues to figure out the meaning of an unfamiliar word. Sometimes authors will restate or explain a concept using different words.

Read this article about the Dust Bowl. Look for clues to the meaning of each boldfaced word. Underline any words that show the author is restating something. Write the meanings on the lines.

In the early 1900s, many people moved onto the Great Plains. These **settlers** farmed the rich soils. They plowed up **native** grasses, that is, those that naturally grew there, and planted wheat instead. For many years, the land **produced** big harvests. But at the start of the Great Depression, wheat prices fell. As a result, many farmers simply **abandoned**, or left, their fields.

In the early 1930s, about half of Americans lived in **rural** areas, meaning in the countryside. At the same time as the Great Depression, a long **drought** began. Without rainfall, crops died and the soil was **exposed**. The grasses that used to grow on the Plains no longer held the soil in place. Strong winds caused soil **erosion**. In other words, the top layer of soil began to blow away. Huge dust storms roared across the prairies. Sometimes dust drifted like snow. Dust storms blackened the skies. The area was called the Dust Bowl. Many farmers lost land and homes. About 400,000 people **migrated**, or left the Plains. Large numbers went west to California hoping for a better life.

1. **Settlers** are _____

2. **Native** means _____

3. **Produced** means _____

4. **Abandoned** means _____

5. **Rural** means _____

6. A **drought** is _____

7. **Exposed** means _____

8. **Erosion** is _____

9. **Migrated** means _____

© New Readers Press. All rights reserved.

7. Parts of Speech and the Dictionary

If you see an unfamiliar word while reading, figure out its part of speech. Is it a noun, verb, adjective, or adverb? If you look the word up in a dictionary, you will need to know the part of speech. Dictionaries list definitions separately for each part of speech that a word can play.

Write the part of speech of each boldfaced word on the short line. Then look up the word in a dictionary and write the definition that matches how the word is used in the sentence.

1. In a stock market **crash**, stocks or shares of companies lose their value quickly.

   _____ _____

2. President Roosevelt passed rules to help keep banks **open** during the Depression.

   _____ _____

3. Companies did not want to **produce** goods that people would not buy.

   _____ _____

4. During the Great Depression, people waited in lines to get **free** soup and bread.

   _____ _____

5. Many people did not think their money was **safe** in banks, so they took it out.

   _____ _____

> An adjective is a word that tells more about a noun or pronoun. Adjectives can come before a noun (the *dusty* road) or after (The road was *dusty*.)

> The pronunciation of *produce* differs depending on whether it is a noun or a verb. noun: PRO-duce; verb: pro-DUCE.

8. Multiple-Meaning Words

Many words have more than one meaning. To figure out the meaning of an unfamiliar word, look at surrounding words and sentences.

Look at each underlined word. Circle the letter of the best definition.

1. In the 1930s, <u>crop</u> prices fell, making it hard for many farmers to survive.
   a. to cut a photo's size
   b. plants that are grown to sell

2. "Bank runs," when many people tried to withdraw all their money, caused some banks to <u>fail</u> in the 1930s.
   a. to not pass a test
   b. to be unable to continue in business

3. Grasses helped hold the <u>rich</u> soils of the Great Plains in place.
   a. having a lot of money
   b. good for growing plants

4. One part of the New Deal protected people's bank <u>deposits</u>.
   a. money that is put into a bank for safekeeping
   b. money that you pay when you rent something

5. Social Security was a New Deal <u>program</u>; it still helps people today.
   a. a plan of activities or measures aimed at a long-term goal
   b. a show that you watch on TV

© New Readers Press. All rights reserved.

Unit 5 Review

Complete each sentence with a word from the list.

expanded	government	produced	program	rural

1. During the 1930s, the U.S. _____ used tax money to pay artists, photographers, teachers, librarians, and others for arts projects.

2. One _____, the Public Works of Art Project (PWAP), paid artists to make paintings, murals, prints, and sculptures for government buildings.

3. In 1934, the PWAP artists _____ over 15,000 works of art.

4. Dorothea Lange worked for the Farm Security Administration and is famous for her photographs. Some of her best photos show poor farmers and _____ life during the Dust Bowl years.

5. In the 1930s, some politicians wanted New Deal arts projects to be ended, but others argued that the programs were good and should be _____.

Choose the best word to finish each sentence. Write it on the line.

6. The _____ grasses that grew on the Great Plains helped hold the soil in place.

   native   **rich**   **free**

7. Arts projects in the 1930s allowed artists to _____ their views about the U.S. and its people.

   depress   **pressure**   **express**

8. The stock market _____ in 1929, when stocks lost much of their value, started the Great Depression.

   recovery   **crash**   **prosperity**

9. Family _____ dropped in the 1930s because people lost their jobs and people with jobs were paid less than before.

   investment   **oppression**   **income**

What do you think would happen if the U.S. had another depression like the one in the 1930s? Write your answer on a separate sheet of paper. Use at least five words you learned in this unit. Circle the vocabulary words you use.

© New Readers Press. All rights reserved.

TESTING TIP:

If a test question asks you about the meaning of a word, see if you can break the word into parts. Do you see any prefixes, suffixes, or roots that you know? Then look at the context of the word. Look for clues in nearby sentences, such as synonyms, examples, or definitions that can help you figure out the meaning.

Circle the letter of the best answer.

1. **Which meaning of *depression* matches how the word is used in this sentence?**

   The U.S. experienced an economic <u>depression</u> from 1893 to 1898, but it was not as severe as the one in the 1930s.

   A an area that is lower that the area around it

   B a state of sadness and feeling hopeless

   C a weather condition with low air pressure

   D a time of low economic activity

2. **What does the word *drought* mean in this sentence?**

   Farmers on the Great Plains were hurt not only by the depression and a drop in prices, but also by a long <u>drought</u> that harmed crops.

   A a period of low spending

   B a time of little or no rain

   C a period of high unemployment

   D a time of great difficulty

3. **Which word means "the act or process of making something better"?**

   A improvement

   B unimproved

   C prove

   D provable

4. **Which word in the passage means about the same as *relief*?**

   One part of the New Deal aimed to give people <u>relief</u>. For example, some people could get cash payments. Others got temporary jobs. One program employed people in national parks and forests.

   A part

   B payments

   C help

   D forests

5. **Which word best completes the sentence?**

   The New Deal included rules for protecting people's bank _____ because many people had lost their money when the banks failed.

   A achievements

   B debt

   C deposits

   D policies

6. **What is the meaning of the word *consumers* as it is used in this sentence?**

   During the Great Depression, <u>consumers</u> worried about the economy and stopped spending.

   A people who invest in stocks and bonds

   B people who buy goods or services

   C people who make products

   D people who grow crops

Check your answers on page 105.

© New Readers Press. All rights reserved.

6 Hoover Dam

VOCABULARY

Read these words from the passage. Check the words you know.

- [ ] annual
- [ ] generate
- [ ] hydroelectric power
- [ ] irrigate
- [ ] source
- [ ] unreliable

Functional Vocabulary

- [ ] prevent

Why Hoover Dam Was Built

Hoover Dam was built between 1931 and 1935 to control the Colorado River and create a regular water supply for several western states. At the time, it was the highest dam in the world.

Before Hoover Dam was built, the Colorado River was dangerous and **unreliable**. Melting mountain snow caused the river to flood in the late spring and early summer. But by mid-summer, the river generally slowed down so much it couldn't supply the water that farmers in the valleys of Arizona and California and the deserts of Nevada needed to **irrigate** their land.

Engineers studied the Colorado River for more than 20 years. They were looking for a place where they could store water from the **annual** spring runoff to **prevent** flooding, and then release the water during the summer when it was needed. They decided that a giant dam on the lower Colorado River was the best solution. During that time, builders in Los Angeles and other growing cities became interested in the dam. They saw the dam as a **source** of water and **hydroelectric power** for homes, businesses, and factories.

Four goals were set for the dam: to prevent floods, to improve navigation on the river, to store and deliver the Colorado's waters, and to **generate** electric power. The bid for the job was just under 49 million dollars and went to a group of six companies that called themselves "Six Companies."

1. Vocabulary Focus

Write each word from the vocabulary list beside its definition.

_____ 1. to stop something from happening

_____ 2. a person, place, or thing from which something comes

_____ 3. to produce (something)

_____ 4. that you cannot trust

_____ 5. electricity created by flowing or falling water

_____ 6. to supply water to land for growing crops

_____ 7. yearly

© New Readers Press. All rights reserved.

What Hoover Dam Does

Hoover Dam was built to provide power and manage the Colorado River. Its construction made possible the development of the Southwest.

The Colorado River is 1,400 miles long and flows through or along seven U.S. states and into Mexico. People had been living in the hot dry land near the Colorado River for thousands of years before Hoover Dam was built. The dam formed Lake Mead, the largest man-made **reservoir** in the U.S. Construction was completed under **budget** and ahead of **schedule**.

Today, the Colorado River supplies drinking water to close to 36 million people, including **residents** of Colorado, Utah, Nevada, Arizona, and California. It creates welcoming **habitats** for a wide **variety** of wildlife. It irrigates close to six million acres of farmland. It supports lots of outdoor and water activities, and it powers the hydroelectric plants at Hoover Dam.

The **primary** purpose of the dam is to generate electricity. The water that goes through the hydroelectric plant creates enough energy to serve more than a million people a year. The water then flows downstream where it can be stored behind other smaller dams and used again. There are over 53 dams on the Colorado River and its branches. The dams all use much of the same water and work together to control the flow of the river.

2. Vocabulary Focus

Read each sentence. Write the word from the vocabulary list that means the same thing as the underlined word or words.

_____ 1. Hoover Dam's planners and designers needed a <u>mix</u> of skills and subject backgrounds.

_____ 2. Construction crews worked so hard on Hoover Dam that they beat their own <u>plan with dates or times when something will happen</u>.

_____ 3. Hoover Dam destroyed the <u>natural homes</u> of some animals and created some new ones.

_____ 4. The construction of Hoover Dam changed the homes and lives of Native American <u>people who live in a particular place.</u>

_____ 5. There are many smaller dams on the Colorado River, but the <u>most important</u> one is Hoover Dam.

_____ 6. The <u>man-made lake</u> formed by Hoover Dam is 110 miles long and 590 feet at its deepest.

_____ 7. Six Companies had a <u>plan of how much money they could spend</u> that they had to keep to.

Read these words from the passage. Check the words you know.

- [ ] budget
- [ ] habitats
- [ ] primary
- [ ] reservoir
- [ ] residents
- [ ] schedule

Functional Vocabulary

- [ ] variety

© New Readers Press. All rights reserved.

3. Work With New Vocabulary

Answer the questions. Explain your answers.

1. Should the government be able to damage the **habitats** of wild animals in order to make life better for people? Explain your answer.

_____

Residents (people) and residence (a person's home) sound the same and look similar, but mean different things.

2. Describe the **residents** of the area where you grew up.

_____

3. During a severe drought [a very long period of time without rain], is it OK to **irrigate** farmland? A public park? A home garden? A front yard? How are these different?

_____

4. Write about something large or small that you were able to **prevent**. Why did you do it? What were the effects?

_____

5. Why was it necessary for Six Companies to work on a **schedule**?

_____

6. Think about someone or something in your life that is **unreliable**. How would you change things if you could?

_____

7. What do you do to **generate** ideas for a paper or project at school or at work?

_____

8. Is it important to you to know the **source** of your food or water? Why or why not?

_____

9. Why is **hydroelectric power** a good or a bad way to create electricity?

_____

10. Describe three things you do **annually**.

_____

11. What are three benefits of studying a **variety** of subjects in school?

_____

12. Who is the **primary** person you talk to about issues at school? At work? At home? Why is that person a good resource for each situation?

_____

© New Readers Press. All rights reserved.

4. Prefix *mid-*

The prefix *mid-* means "middle." You can combine *mid-* with nouns to form new words. For example, *mid- + night = midnight*.

Complete each sentence with a word from the list. If you aren't sure of a word's meaning, look it up in the dictionary.

> The prefix *mid-* uses a hyphen before a capitalized word (*mid-Atlantic*) or a number (*mid-1930s*).

mid-1930s	mid-August	midterm	midtown	midway	Midwest

1. There are about 28,000 dams in the _____.

2. The good thing about _____ exams is that you already know half of what you're going to learn in the course.

3. The committee to discuss the new city power plant met in _____ last week.

4. Hoover Dam was dedicated in the _____.

5. The hottest weather recorded at Hoover Dam was in _____.

6. _____ through the governor's speech, several people left the room in protest.

5. Suffixes *-able, -ible*

The suffixes *-able* and *-ible* mean "is" and "able to be." When you add one of them to a verb, the verb becomes an adjective. If the verb ends in *e*, you usually drop the *e* before adding the suffix. But you keep the final *e* when it's attached to a soft *c* or *g*, as in *noticeable* and *manageable*.

Add the suffix -able or -ible to make an adjective of each item. Write the adjectives on the lines.

> If you're adding the suffix to a complete word, the ending is almost always *-able*.

1. afford _____

2. poss _____

3. profit _____

4. change _____

5. compare _____

6. vis _____

The underlined word in each sentence has the suffix -able or -ible. Write the definition of the underlined word. Use a dictionary to check your answers.

7. The land around Hoover Dam is quite <u>valuable</u>, but it is not for sale.

   definition: _____

8. Could you hear what the engineer said? I thought he was barely <u>audible</u>.

   definition: _____

9. Hoover Dam regulates the flow of water and creates a <u>dependable</u> water supply for much of the Southwest.

   definition: _____

© New Readers Press. All rights reserved.

6. Context Clues: General Clues, Definitions, and Examples

When you're trying to determine the meaning of a new word, it can be helpful to look at what comes before and after that word. There may be examples, definitions, or synonyms.

Read the paragraphs. Look for clues to help you understand the meaning of each boldfaced word. Write the meaning on the line.

The federal government had plans to build a town for dam workers. But because of the Depression, many workers arrived in Nevada long before work on the dam began. They lived in temporary **makeshift** tent camps. Life wasn't easy in "Ragtown," with no electricity and poor health and **sanitary** conditions. Temperatures sometimes reached 120 degrees.

The federal government and Six Companies built Boulder City to provide **suitable** and acceptable housing for the men and their families. Boulder City included housing and stores, and took care of the general health and happiness or **welfare** of the community by providing a post office, churches, and schools.

1. **Makeshift** means _____

2. To be **sanitary** means to be _____

3. If something is **suitable**, it is _____

4. **Welfare** means _____

> Most vocabulary words are learned in context.

There are several helpful ways to use context to figure out the meaning of a word. The first is to look and see if the definition of the word is right there. Also look for a synonym or related words.

Underline definitions, synonyms, or related words that help explain each boldfaced word. Then write a definition. Check your answers in a dictionary.

5. Hoover Dam is 726.4 feet high from its **foundation** to the top. It's 660 feet thick at the base and 45 feet thick at the top.

   definition: _____

6. Before Hoover Dam was built, the area was **desolate**. It was lonely desert land with few people.

   definition: _____

7. The Great Depression caused a **massive** migration of men hoping to get jobs. Large numbers of workers arrived in Nevada years before dam construction began.

   definition: _____

8. Hoover Dam protects southern California and Arizona from the **disastrous** floods that had damaged parts of the Imperial and Palo Verde Valleys in the past.

   definition: _____

© New Readers Press. All rights reserved.

7. Parts of Speech and the Dictionary

Understanding the parts of speech and how they fit together makes writing and reading easier. All words have a part of speech according to the part they play in a sentence.

Look at each boldfaced word. What part of speech does it play? Circle noun *or* verb. *Then look up the word in a dictionary. Write the correct definition on the line.*

noun   verb   1. In 1932, the government built Boulder City to **house** some of the men working on Hoover Dam.

_____

noun   verb   2. The Hoover Dam power plant began **service** on September 12, 1936.

_____

noun   verb   3. Some men had to **desert** their families during the Depression to find work; however, many men moved to the Hoover Dam area with their families.

_____

noun   verb   4. Parts of Hoover Dam were designed to **honor** the Native American cultures of the area.

_____

noun   verb   5. After all these years, Hoover Dam is still considered an engineering **wonder**.

_____

> ● When *house* is a noun, it rhymes with *mouse*. When it is a verb, *house* rhymes with *cows*.

> ● A lot of people mix up the spelling of *desert* and *dessert*. Just remember that *dessert* with *ss* is the "sweet stuff" you eat at the end of a meal.

8. Multiple-Meaning Words

A multiple-meaning word has several meanings that are listed under one entry in a dictionary. The meanings may be for the same or different parts of speech.

Look at each underlined word. Circle the letter of the best definition.

1. Can you believe that Hoover Dam is 60 <u>stories</u> high?
   a. reports of events
   b. levels in a building

2. The <u>initial</u> plan was to build Hoover Dam at Boulder Canyon about 10 miles north of Black Canyon where it is actually located.
   a. first letter of a person's name
   b. first

3. When you <u>dam</u> up a river, everything from lakes to islands can be created.
   a. stop the flow of water
   b. a barrier stopping the flow of water

4. In the summer, temperatures reached 120 degrees in the canyon. There was no <u>shade</u>.
   a. an area of darkness and coolness caused by blocking out the Sun
   b. how light or dark a color is

> ● The more you read, the easier it is to determine and remember the meaning of a multiple-meaning word.

© New Readers Press. All rights reserved.

Unit 6 Review

Choose the best word to complete each sentence. Write it on the line.

1. Hoover Dam was built in a _____, wild, and hot area.

   Midwest   **desert**   **desolate**

2. It is as tall as a 60-story building. Its _____ is as thick as two football fields are long.

   foundation   **reservoir**   **habitat**

3. Lake Mead is _____, holding almost 29 million acre-feet of water.

   comparable   **massive**   **makeshift**

4. It stores water that _____ two million acres in southern California and across the state line in Arizona.

   houses   **dams**   **irrigates**

5. The land around Lake Mead has become a natural _____ for all kinds of animals.

   reservoir   **source**   **habitat**

Circle the letter of the answer that best completes each sentence.

6. If something is **sanitary**, it is _____.
   a. clean
   b. primary
   c. unreliable

7. When a dam **prevents flooding**, it _____.
   a. stops the rain
   b. irrigates the fields
   c. controls the water

8. **Hydroelectric power** generates _____.
   a. shade
   b. stories
   c. electricity

9. If a job is of **primary** importance, it _____.
   a. is done every year
   b. should be done first
   c. was already done

Explain the importance of Hoover Dam. Write your answer on a separate sheet of paper. Use at least five words you learned in this unit. Circle the vocabulary words you use.

© New Readers Press. All rights reserved.

© New Readers Press. All rights reserved.

TESTING TIP:

When you're having difficulty choosing between two multiple-choice answer options, ask yourself which choice more completely answers the question. That is probably the right answer.

Circle the letter of the best answer.

1. **Which words in the passage mean about the same as *residents*?**

   During the construction of Hoover Dam, the residents of Boulder City all had steady jobs and houses. The people who lived there made the city their home. Businesses included restaurants, a movie theatre, and a variety of stores.

   A steady jobs

   B the people who lived there

   C their home

   D a variety of stores

2. **Which of the following words means "can be changed"?**

   A changing

   B changeable

   C changable

   D changed

3. **What does the word *initial* mean in this sentence?**

   The initial plans for Boulder City changed because of the Great Depression.

   A at the beginning of something

   B sign something with your initials

   C an extra-large letter at the beginning of a story or a chapter in a book

   D the first letter of a proper name

4. **What does the word *budget* mean in this passage?**

   If you're traveling to Las Vegas, budget time to visit Hoover Dam. It's worth the money. Over a million people take the trip every year.

   A make and follow a plan for spending money

   B a plan to decide how much money to spend and how to spend it

   C low in price

   D plan how to use something

5. **What is the meaning of *source* as it is used in this sentence?**

   Having family with them was a great source of comfort to many of the men doing the hard and dangerous work of building Hoover Dam.

   A where something comes from

   B someone who starts something

   C a person, book, etc. that gives information

   D the beginning of a stream or river of water

6. **Which of the following is an example of the *mid-1930s*?**

   A 1915

   B 1930

   C 1935

   D 1950

Check your answers beginning on page 105.

7 Ecosystems

© New Readers Press. All rights reserved.

VOCABULARY

Read these words from the passage. Check the words you know.

☐ biomes

☐ climate

☐ precipitation

☐ species

☐ survive

☐ vegetation

Functional Vocabulary

☐ defined

The Sonoran Desert

You might think all deserts are hot, sandy, and bare. But the Sonoran Desert is full of plant and animal life.

A desert is **defined** by low annual **precipitation**. Deserts are arid, or dry. When rain does fall, it usually evaporates quickly. It may seem that a desert would be a hard place to **survive** in. But many plants and animals thrive in these dry conditions.

The Sonoran Desert, which includes parts of California, Arizona, and the state of Sonora, Mexico, is a good example. This desert is unique because of the natural variation that occurs there. Visitors to the Sonoran Desert might be surprised by the amount of **vegetation** they see. The desert is home to more than 2,000 **species** of plants. It's also home to more than 350 species of birds as well as many kinds of mammals, reptiles, amphibians, and even fish. Even the soil crust in the desert is alive with living organisms.

There are several **biomes**, or large areas defined by **climate** and plant life, within the Sonoran Desert. These biomes range from desert, where plants like cacti grow, to grasslands, to forests with pines, oaks, and other trees. The Sonoran Desert has mild winters with gentle rains and late summers with heavy storms. These weather patterns allow a diversity of plant and animals to survive there. The area may be dry, but it is definitely not empty or lifeless.

1. Vocabulary Focus

Complete each sentence with a word from the vocabulary list.

1. Water that falls to the ground in the form of rain or snow is

   _____.

2. The plants that are found in an area are its _____.

3. A region's _____ is its weather pattern.

4. When something is _____, it is shown or described clearly.

5. When animals _____, they stay alive.

6. A _____ is a group into which plants or animals can be divided.

7. A _____ is a region on Earth with a defined type of weather, plants, and animals.

The Galápagos Islands

The Galápagos Islands are famous as the place where Charles Darwin began to form ideas that changed how humans saw themselves and the world around them.

The Galápagos Islands, which lie about 600 miles west of South America, are sometimes called a "living laboratory." The islands were formed by volcanoes. Even though the islands are **similar** in **composition** and climate, each island **ecosystem** has its own unique species, including birds and giant tortoises.

Charles Darwin visited the islands in 1835. Darwin was a naturalist, a scientist who studied the natural world. He studied the geology as well as the biology of the islands, collecting specimens as he traveled. Darwin collected samples of finches, small songbirds. After Darwin returned to London, he realized that the birds were similar but had different kinds of beaks. Darwin **concluded** that the finches had all come from a single ancestor species and had changed over time. Over many years, the birds **adapted** to the specific foods available in their own island ecosystems. Their beaks became specialized to eat different foods like seeds, insects, or flowers. The single ancestor species had become 14 different finch species on the Galápagos Islands.

Years later, Darwin used his research from the Galápagos Islands when he developed his **theory** of **evolution**.

2. Vocabulary Focus

Write each word from the vocabulary list beside its definition.

_____ 1. the nature of something's parts or ingredients

_____ 2. almost the same

_____ 3. formed an opinion after careful thought and research

_____ 4. changed to make it easier to live in a place or situation

_____ 5. all the living and nonliving things that are in a particular environment

_____ 6. a set of related ideas that are intended to explain something

_____ 7. a process in which living things change over time in response to their environments

VOCABULARY

Read these words from the passage. Check the words you know.

☐ adapted

☐ composition

☐ ecosystem

☐ evolution

☐ similar

☐ theory

Functional Vocabulary

☐ concluded

© New Readers Press. All rights reserved.

3. Work With New Vocabulary

Complete each idea. Write your answer on the line.

1. When a lot of **precipitation** falls in a short time, _____

   _____

2. Things that you could find in an **ecosystem** include _____

   _____

3. To **survive** in a cold **climate**, you would need _____

   _____

4. Darwin formed his **theory** of **evolution** by _____

   _____

5. Animals might **adapt** to their environment by _____

   _____

Answer the questions. Explain your answers.

The word *vegetation* starts with the root *veg*. Use the meaning of a familiar word like *vegetable*, which has the same root, to help you figure out the meaning of *vegetation*.

6. Would you be likely to see more **vegetation** in a desert **biome** or in a forest biome? Explain.

   _____

7. How would you **define** a desert? An island?

   _____

8. Is a pond **similar** to an ocean? Explain your answer.

   _____

9. What would you **conclude** if it didn't rain for a year where you live?

   _____

10. Describe the **composition** of your class or household.

   _____

The letter *c* in *species* makes the *sh* sound.

11. Cats and dogs are both mammals. Are they in the same **species**? Explain your answer.

   _____

© New Readers Press. All rights reserved.

4. Suffixes -logy, -logist

The suffix *-logy* means "the science of" or "the study of." The suffix *-logist* means "one who studies."

The roots in the list can be combined with the suffixes -ology and -ologist to form words. Write the word that completes each sentence. The first one is done for you. Check a dictionary if you are unsure of the spelling.

Words that end with the suffix *-ist* name a person who does an action. *Dentist, florist,* and *scientist* are some examples.

anthropo = people; culture		audio = hearing		bio = life
cardio = heart	dermato = skin	geo = Earth		zoo = animal

1. Martha went to see an _____*audiologist*_____ to have her hearing checked.

2. A _____ is a doctor who is an expert in treating heart disease.

3. If you want to work with wildlife or animals living in an ecosystem, study _____.

4. _____ is the study of human customs, cultures, and beliefs.

5. A _____ can study many different kinds of life, including bacteria, cells, plants, and animals.

6. Some people study _____ so that they know where the best places are to drill for oil or mine minerals.

7. _____ is a branch of medicine that deals with caring for the skin.

5. Suffix -al

The suffix *-al* can mean "relating to" or "characterized by" when it is added to a noun to make an adjective. For example, the noun *occasion* + the suffix *-al* = *occasional*, an adjective that means "happening sometimes, but not often."

Complete each sentence with a word from the list.

The suffix *-al* can also be added to some verbs to make nouns. For example: *survival, rehearsal, approval.*

annual	national	natural	nocturnal	seasonal	tropical

1. Many desert animals are _____ because temperatures are too hot during the day.

2. The Galápagos Islands have _____ weather. The weather is warm and wet because the islands are near the equator.

3. The _____ rainfall in a desert is less than 10 inches per year.

4. There are several _____ parks and forests that people can visit to experience the Sonoran Desert. These parks are owned and protected by the federal government.

5. The Sonoran Desert has a _____ rainfall pattern. It usually rains in winter and in late summer.

6. Today many people visit the Galápagos Islands. They hope to see unusual wildlife in its _____ habitat.

© New Readers Press. All rights reserved.

6. Context Clues: Definitions and General Clues

The words *is, are, means, meaning,* and *or* can be clues that an author is defining a word.

An author may define a scientific or technical term. If you see an unfamiliar word or term, keep reading to see if the author defines it. If not, look for other clues in the context to figure out the word's meaning.

Read the passage about invasive species. Look for clues to the meaning of each boldfaced word. Some of the words are defined in the paragraph. Complete the definitions.

Invasive species can harm ecosystems, including the plants, animals, and people who live there. A species is invasive when it is not native, or naturally found, in an environment. Invasive species can **disrupt** ecosystems. This means that they interrupt the way things normally work.

Invasive species might **prey** on, or hunt and eat, native species. For example, in southern Florida, Burmese pythons (a kind of snake from Southeast Asia) caused some bird and rat species to **decline**, or go down in number. Invasive species also **compete** with native species for food and other **resources** like sunlight or water. Asian carp (a large fish) harm native fish in American rivers. Invasive species can **thrive** in some ecosystems because nothing preys on or eats them. Then these species can **reproduce** and spread quickly.

Invasive species can also cause an animal species to become **extinct**, which means the species is no longer alive. Dodo birds, for example, lived on the island of Mauritius. Sailors who arrived in the 1600s hunted the birds. But they also brought dogs, cats, and pigs that ate the eggs and the young birds. Within 80 years, all dodos were dead.

1. A species is **invasive** when _____

2. To **disrupt** means _____

The words *prey* and *pray* sound the same but have different meanings. To *pray* means "to speak to a god to give thanks or ask for something."

3. When species **prey**, they _____

4. When species **decline**, they _____

5. To **compete** means _____

6. **Resources** are _____

7. To **thrive** means _____

8. When species **reproduce**, they _____

9. **Extinct** means _____

© New Readers Press. All rights reserved.

7. Parts of Speech and the Dictionary

Dictionaries list the part of speech next to each entry word. If a word can play more than one part in speech, most dictionaries will show a separate entry for each possibility. If a word has more than one definition, definitions will be numbered.

On the short line, write the part of speech of each boldfaced word. Then look up the word in a dictionary and write the definition that matches how the word is used in the sentence.

1. The **state** of Arizona has parts of all four of the major North American deserts.

   _____ _____

2. Weather **conditions** in the Sonoran Desert allow many kinds of plants to grow there.

   _____ _____

3. The **main** rainy season in the Sonoran Desert is July through September, when warm, wet air moves through the region.

   _____ _____

4. Islands can **form** when underwater volcanoes erupt.

   _____ _____

5. The Rub al Khali is a large **empty** desert in Arabia; some people describe it as a "sea of sand."

   _____ _____

8. Multiple-Meaning Words

A word can have more than one meaning. Think about a word's context to figure out the correct meaning. You can also check the different meanings in a dictionary.

Look at each underlined word. Circle the letter of the best definition.

1. Plants in the desert <u>range</u> from grasses to cacti to trees.
   a. vary from one thing to another thing
   b. to move around an area

2. The desert soil <u>crust</u> may look like dirt, but it actually contains living things.
   a. the outer edges of bread
   b. a hard surface layer

3. Some forests in the southern Sonora Desert are lush and green in the summer rainy season but <u>bare</u> the other nine months of the year.
   a. without leaves or plants
   b. not covered with clothes

4. Three ocean <u>currents</u> meet near the Galápagos Islands.
   a. the flow of electricity
   b. water moving continuously in one direction

5. Weather <u>patterns</u> influence the kinds of plants that grow on the Galápagos Islands.
   a. regular ways that something happens over and over again
   b. shapes or models that are used to make something

Many dictionaries show an example for each meaning of a word. When you look up a multiple-meaning word, use these to find the definition that matches how your word is being used.

Don't confuse the words *bear* and *bare*, which sound the same. The word *bear* can mean "a large furry animal" or "to accept or deal with."

© New Readers Press. All rights reserved.

Unit 7 Review

Circle the letter of the answer that best completes each sentence.

1. A person who studies **geology** would most likely be studying _____.
   a. weather and climate patterns
   b. the materials Earth is made of
   c. human cultures and traditions

2. If a plant species is **invasive**, it _____.
   a. grows to a very large size
   b. is not native to an ecosystem
   c. needs little water

3. An **annual** event happens _____.
   a. once a day
   b. once a month
   c. once a year

4. A **nocturnal** animal is one that _____.
   a. preys on other animals
   b. lives in the desert
   c. is active at night

Choose the best word to complete each sentence. Write it on the line.

5. A desert _____ includes all of the things that live there, such as plants and animals, as well as nonliving things, such as the soil, rocks, water, and weather.

   climate   **resource**   **ecosystem**

6. Dinosaurs became _____ millions of years ago. But other animals, such as the passenger pigeon, completely died out only about 100 years ago.

   empty   **similar**   **extinct**

7. Finches on the Galápagos Islands were able to _____ only if they had the right kind of beak for eating the available food.

   decline   **survive**   **disrupt**

8. Charles Darwin studied the _____ world. From 1831 to 1836, he traveled the globe and filled dozens of notebooks with observations about plants, animals, and geology.

   seasonal   **biome**   **natural**

What kind of ecosystem would you like to live in? Describe it in as much detail as you can. Write your answer on a separate sheet of paper. Use at least five words you learned in this unit. Circle the vocabulary words you use.

© New Readers Press. All rights reserved.

© New Readers Press. All rights reserved.

TESTING TIP:

Some test questions will ask about a word's meaning. Find the word in the reading passage and reread the paragraph where the word appears. Look for context clues to help you. Does the author use a synonym (word that means almost the same), give a definition, or provide examples? These clues can help you figure out the meaning.

Circle the letter of the best answer.

1. **Which meaning of *conditions* matches how the word is used in this sentence?**

   Conditions in the Sonoran Desert can be harsh, with summer temperatures often reaching 118°F.

   A the type of weather at a certain time

   B the state of a person's health

   C rules that you must agree to

   D illnesses or medical problems

2. **What does the word *adapted* mean in this passage?**

   Many animals have adapted to living in hot deserts. For example, jackrabbits have large ears that let body heat escape.

   A learned how to stay warm

   B moved to cooler places

   C split into different groups

   D changed to fit a new situation

3. **Which meaning of *composition* matches how the word is used in this passage?**

   The composition of desert soil crust is interesting. It can include mosses, lichen, and bacteria.

   A the process of putting words and pictures on a page before printing it

   B a short piece of writing

   C the parts that something is made up of

   D the way subjects are arranged in a photo

4. **Which of the following is an example of *precipitation*?**

   A sand

   B rain

   C sunlight

   D climate

5. **Which word best completes the passage?**

   Plants and animals got to the Galápagos Islands by air or by water. Strong storms blew some birds and seeds to the islands, while good swimmers like sea turtles and penguins got there with the help of ocean _____.

   A currents

   B ranges

   C species

   D climates

6. **What word in the passage means about the same as *vegetation*?**

   The vegetation on the Galápagos Islands is less diverse than what is found on the South American continent. The islands have a lot of ferns and grasses, but few plants that have large seeds or big flowers.

   A diverse

   B continent

   C plants

   D seeds

Check your answers on page 106.

8 Animal Behavior

VOCABULARY

Read these words from the passage. Check the words you know.

- ☐ flexible
- ☐ innate
- ☐ interact
- ☐ mammals
- ☐ predators
- ☐ predictable

Functional Vocabulary

- ☐ combine

Innate Behavior and Learned Behavior

Animal behavior is anything an animal does and how it does it. This behavior may take place when the animal is alone or with other animals.

Animals do the things they do in order to find food and water, **interact** in social groups, keep away from **predators**, and have and raise their young.

Innate behaviors, such as yawning and blinking, don't have to be learned or practiced. They are ways animals behave naturally. Innate behaviors are **predictable**—all members of a species perform innate behaviors the same way and do them well the first time they try.

While some animal behaviors are innate, many are learned from practice and experience. Learning occurs gradually and in steps. Animals often learn by observing or watching the behavior of other animals. Young monkeys, for example, learn to wash their food by copying older monkeys. Learned behavior is **flexible**; it can change if conditions change. Most animal behaviors **combine** innate behavior and learned behavior.

Social behaviors are interactions between members of the same species. For many species, play is an important way of training for life, especially for developing physical skills. Most young **mammals** learn the skills they will need as adults through play. When you watch kittens play with a toy and toss it in the air or chase each other, you're watching them learn to hunt.

1. Vocabulary Focus

Complete each sentence with a word from the vocabulary list.

1. Something is _____ if it is natural and inborn.

2. When you _____ things, they are blended or joined together.

3. _____ are the group of animals that feed milk to their young.

4. If something is _____, it is able to change.

5. _____ are animals that live by killing and eating other animals.

6. When animals _____, the actions of each one in a group affect the actions of others.

7. If something is _____, you know what will happen before it takes place.

© New Readers Press. All rights reserved.

Intelligent Behavior, Social Behavior, and Communication

Animal behaviorism is the scientific study of animal behavior.

Most animals **exhibit** some kind of social behavior. Many live in close groups with other members of their species. Each member of a group has a specific **role** to play. Group members cooperate to raise their young, hunt, and defend themselves. Social behavior helps a species succeed and survive. Baby raccoons, for example, learn to climb trees (and stay away from predators) by **imitating** other raccoons and copying what they do.

Wolves and fish are very social. They live and work together for the good of the group. Dolphins have an especially strong sense of social identity. They know who they are and who and where their groups are. They **comprehend** the health and feelings of other dolphins. On the other hand, some animals, such as polar bears, rarely interact with others of their species.

Social animals need to communicate. Animals can communicate with sounds, chemicals, or **visual signals**. Frogs, some reptiles, and almost all mammals and birds use sound to communicate. For example, dolphins and whales make a wide variety of underwater sounds. Ants communicate by marking the path to a food supply with chemicals so that other ants can find the way. Bees show the location of food by performing a **specialized** dance.

2. Vocabulary Focus

Write a word from the vocabulary list that means that same thing as the underlined text.

_____ 1. What <u>sound, action, or event that gives information</u> did the dog give to tell you that he was hungry?

_____ 2. Fireflies that glow at night are communicating to each other with <u>related to seeing</u> signals.

_____ 3. Baby killer whales learn by following their mothers and <u>copying the way they behave and move</u> what they do.

_____ 4. Most people can't <u>understand</u> how animals communicate with each other.

_____ 5. Every honey bee in a community has a <u>designed for one particular purpose</u> job.

_____ 6. A dog often has trouble understanding its <u>position, job, or function</u> in the family when its owners bring home another dog.

_____ 7. A cat will <u>show</u> happiness when its eyes are wide open and its mouth is closed and relaxed.

© New Readers Press. All rights reserved.

VOCABULARY

Read these words from the passage. Check the words you know.

- ☐ comprehend
- ☐ imitating
- ☐ role
- ☐ signals
- ☐ specialized
- ☐ visual

Functional Vocabulary

- ☐ exhibit

3. Work With New Vocabulary

Write T *if a statement is true. Write* F *if the statement is false and explain why it is false.*

1. _____ Writing is an **innate** behavior in humans.

   _____

2. _____ Butterflies make excellent **predators**.

   _____

3. _____ An animal that acts in a **predictable** way behaves in a way that surprises you.

   _____

4. _____ Some animal behaviorists **specialize** in wolves. They study how wolves hunt, travel, raise their young, and sleep.

   _____

5. _____ A bird singing is an example of a **visual** behavior.

   _____

6. _____ Birds, fish, and reptiles are all **mammals**.

   _____

7. _____ A cat's purr **combines** an innate behavior and a learned behavior.

   _____

Answer the questions. Explain your answers.

In this case, *signal* is a noun, but it can also be used as a verb. For example, *Bees signal the location of the best flowers to other members of the community.*

8. What are three different **signals** people give when they want to end a conversation?

   _____

9. Describe two ways that **imitating** someone or something can help you succeed.

   _____

10. Why is it a good thing to be **flexible** sometimes?

    _____

11. What **role** do you play in your family? What do you do in that role?

    _____

12. Would you rather **interact** with one person at a time or in a group? Explain your answer.

    _____

13. Is it easier for you to **comprehend** something you hear or something you see? Give an example.

    _____

14. What are two ways that people **exhibit** fear?

    _____

© New Readers Press. All rights reserved.

4. Prefixes co-, com-, con-

The prefixes co-, com-, and con- mean "together, with." For example, when you connect things, you join them together. The prefix con- usually becomes com- before b, h, l, m, p, and r, so a group of people that works together is a committee.

Complete each sentence with a word from the list. If you aren't sure of a word's meaning, look it up in the dictionary.

coexist	compete	complicated	construct

1. Honey bees communicate with each other to find the best place to _____ their hives.

2. The relationship between humans and their pets is very _____.

3. Animals often have to _____ against other animals for territory or food.

4. Some dolphins _____ peacefully with whales and other species of dolphins, but they generally avoid sharks.

Write your own sentences with these words that begin with co- *or* com-.

5. contact: _____

6. compare: _____

7. cooperate: _____

5. Roots act, ag

The roots act and ag mean "to do" and "to act." An action is something you do. An agency is a business or department that does a particular job.

Match each word to its definition. Write the letter of the correct definition on the line.

_____ 1. activity   a. to take a number or amount away from something else

_____ 2. agenda   b. a person who represents another person or company

_____ 3. subtract   c. to disturb or excite

_____ 4. agent   d. a list of all the things to be discussed in a meeting

_____ 5. attract   e. a lot of things happening and people doing things

_____ 6. agitate   f. to cause someone or something to come somewhere by offering something of interest

Con is also a word on its own. As a noun, it can mean a "disadvantage" or a "trick." As a verb, it means "to trick someone, especially for money."

© New Readers Press. All rights reserved.

6. Context Clues: Definitions and General Clues

Ask yourself questions to focus your thinking on the possible clues to the meaning of a new word. Ask, *What are the surrounding words and phrases? What information are they giving me?*

When you come across an unknown word, look for a definition hidden in the text. Punctuation like commas, dashes, or semicolons and helping words such as *or* and *like* tell you there's a definition nearby.

Read the paragraph. Look for clues to help you understand the meaning of each boldfaced word. Then write its definition.

In the late 1970s, graduate student Irene Pepperberg decided to **conduct** research into animal intelligence. She went to a pet store in Chicago and bought an African Gray **parrot**. She named the one-year-old bird, "Alex," short for Avian [relating to birds] Learning Experiment. At that time, scientists had few **expectations**, beliefs that something will happen, that a bird could communicate with humans.

Over the next 30 years, Dr. Pepperberg did new and **innovative** research with Alex to learn about animal intelligence. Their work was unique and creative. Alex learned to count, add, and subtract; to **recognize** and identify shapes, sizes, and colors; and to speak, and understand, more than 100 English words.

1. When scientists **conduct** research, they _____

2. A **parrot** is a kind of _____

3. **Expectations** are _____

4. If something is **innovative**, it is _____

5. When you **recognize** a person or a thing, you _____

Underline any clues that help explain the boldfaced words. Then write a definition for each one. Check your answers in a dictionary.

6. Animals may **modify** their behavior in order to adapt to a change in the environment.

   definition: _____

7. Some animals give off a **scent**, or smell, that can be identified by others.

   definition: _____

8. Alex didn't just **memorize** words. He didn't just learn and remember. He understood.

   definition: _____

9. Alex learned to communicate, but he never developed the **linguistic**—the language—abilities of a young child learning to speak.

   definition: _____

10. You can learn more about Alex's **accomplishments** (the things that he did well) in the film, *Life with Alex.*

    definition: _____

© New Readers Press. All rights reserved.

7. Parts of Speech and the Dictionary

You need to know the part or parts of speech a word can play so that you can use it correctly in various contexts. Look for learning cues, such as word endings or position in the sentence, that can help you identify the part of speech.

On the short line, write the part of speech of each boldfaced word. Then look up the word in a dictionary and write the definition that matches how the word is used in the sentence.

1. Dr. Pepperberg used **novel** methods to teach Alex.

   _____ _____

2. Dr. Pepperberg worked with Alex for most of his life and published many reports about his **progress**.

   _____ _____

3. Alex got jelly beans, wood blocks, and other things he liked as **rewards** for answering correctly.

   _____ _____

4. When he was 31 years old, Alex died of natural **causes**. His last words were, "You be good, see you tomorrow. I love you."

   _____ _____

5. Since then, no parrot has been able to perform tasks as **complex** as the ones Alex could.

   _____ _____

> When *progress* is a verb, the stress is on the second syllable, pro-GRESS. When it's used as a noun, it's PRO-gress, with the stress on the first syllable.

8. Multiple-Meaning Words

Choose the correct definition for a multiple-meaning word based on the context of the sentence. Understanding how a multiple meaning word works in a sentence makes it easier to choose the right meaning.

Look at each underlined word. Circle the letter of the best definition.

1. Examples of social groups include schools of fish and <u>packs</u> of wolves.
   a. a group of people
   b. a group of animals that live together

2. Some animals <u>mark</u> the way to a food source.
   a. make or leave a mark on (something)
   b. take notice of

3. It's <u>clear</u> that animals communicate in many ways.
   a. easy to understand, hear, or see
   b. easy to see through

4. Irene Pepperberg was a <u>graduate</u> student when she bought Alex.
   a. someone who has successfully completed her studies at school
   b. relating to study for a master's degree or Ph.D.

5. Some animal behaviorists study how animals <u>rear</u> their young.
   a. raise and care for
   b. rise up on back legs

© New Readers Press. All rights reserved.

Unit 8 Review

Write the pair of words that best completes each sentence.

1. Some birds use their feathers as _____ to _____ other birds.

   scents   **signals**   **attract**   **construct**

2. Ants have specific _____ in their societies, and they _____ with each other to get things done.

   roles   **rewards**   **memorize**   **cooperate**

3. Being _____ makes it possible to _____ to various environments.

   flexible   **specialized**   **adapt**   **recognize**

4. Young children, like other young _____, learn by _____ their parents.

   predators   **mammals**   **imitating**   **antagonizing**

5. Different species of animals can _____ if they don't _____ for food.

   coexist   **compare**   **conduct**   **compete**

Circle the letter of the answer that best completes each sentence.

6. If something is **innovative**, it has probably _____.
   a. won an award
   b. never been done before
   c. been put inside another thing

7. People who study **linguistics** are interested in _____.
   a. languages
   b. business
   c. parrots

8. A **predictable** behavior _____.
   a. happens in a way you expect
   b. is different every time
   c. is memorized

9. Animals that travel in **packs** _____.
   a. carry other animals
   b. live in small spaces
   c. hunt as a group

Why is it important for scientists to study animal behavior? Write your answer on a separate sheet of paper. In your answer, use at least five words you learned in this unit. Circle the vocabulary words you use.

© New Readers Press. All rights reserved.

© New Readers Press. All rights reserved.

TESTING TIP:

People who write multiple-choice tests write answer options that seem reasonable in order to distract you from the correct answer. The key to answering multiple-choice test items correctly is to pay attention to details. Read each item and its answer choices carefully. Remember that you are looking for the *best* answer available.

Circle the letter of the best answer.

1. **Which words in the passage mean about the same as *conduct*?**

   Many animal behaviorists <u>conduct</u> their research in labs. They direct and manage their work at aquariums, universities, and zoos. They identify and study behaviors in order to better understand the various ways animals develop and behave.

   A direct and manage

   B identify and study

   C better understand

   D develop and behave

2. **What does the word *progress* mean in this sentence?**

   The sick bird made a little <u>progress</u> every day.

   A the process of improving

   B movement toward a place

   C movement forward in time

   D the process of happening

3. **Which of the following is something you can be proud of?**

   A an agenda

   B an expectation

   C an accomplishment

   D a scent

4. **What is the meaning of *mark* as it is used in this sentence?**

   House cats and wild cats <u>mark</u> territory in the same way.

   A represent something

   B show where something is or was

   C take notice of

   D measure a student's work

5. **Which definition of *causes* matches the meaning in this passage?**

   Changes in the environment impact the animals that live there. Some of the <u>causes</u> of change are lack of water, lack of food, a difference in temperature, and human activity.

   A people or things that lead to actions, events, or conditions

   B ideas that people care deeply about and want to support

   C reasons for doing something

   D the base for legal action

6. **Which of the following words means "not simple"?**

   A compare

   B construct

   C cooperate

   D complex

Check your answers beginning on page 106.

9 Earth's Changing Surface

© New Readers Press. All rights reserved.

VOCABULARY

Read these words from the passage. Check the words you know.

- ☐ compress
- ☐ dense
- ☐ erode
- ☐ elevations
- ☐ glacier
- ☐ gradual

Functional Vocabulary

- ☐ created

Glaciers

Glaciers have slowly shaped the surface of the Earth. You may not have seen a glacier, but you have probably seen land shaped by one.

A **glacier** is a large sheet of slowly moving ice. A glacier can vary from the size of a football field to more than 100 miles long. Today about 10 percent of Earth's land is covered by glaciers. Glaciers are important because they provide water for people and crops. They also store about 69 percent of Earth's freshwater. If too many glaciers melt, sea levels will rise. Many coastal areas will be flooded.

Glaciers form in places where snow remains on the ground year-round, such as polar regions or high **elevations**. The snow accumulates, or builds up, over time. As more snow falls, the older layers of snow **compress**. The fluffy snow becomes a **dense** mass of ice.

The weight of thick ice causes a glacier to flow very slowly. A glacier's **gradual** movement can reshape the land below. For example, glaciers **created** the U.S.'s Great Lakes, formed valleys, and cut through mountains. Some glaciers carve away rock. As they move, they pick up boulders and gravel and drag them along. This can leave scratches on rock and can **erode** rock surfaces. Sometimes glaciers deposit the materials they carry far from their original locations.

1. Vocabulary Focus

Complete each sentence with a word from the vocabulary list.

1. When you _____ something, you press or squeeze it into a smaller space.

2. When something is _____, it happens slowly over a long time.

3. If you _____ something, you made it happen or exist.

4. Heights above sea level are _____.

5. A _____ is a large area of ice that moves very slowly.

6. To _____ means to slowly destroy the surface of something.

7. An object with parts that are pushed tightly together is _____.

Volcanoes

Volcanoes have changed Earth's surface. They have also affected its air and climate.

Scientists **classify** volcanoes in different ways. Sometimes they group volcanoes by size, shape, or lava type. Another way to classify volcanoes is by level of activity. Active volcanoes **erupt** regularly. Dormant volcanoes erupted in the last several thousand years but are not active now. Extinct volcanoes probably won't erupt again.

What makes an active volcano erupt? Deep inside the Earth, thick melted rock called magma rises toward the surface. When a volcano erupts, magma is pushed through one or more **vents** on Earth's surface. Magma that reaches the surface is called lava.

Sometimes magma is thin and runny. It flows slowly out of a volcano and can create **landforms** such as mountains, layers of rock, or island chains. At other times the magma is too thick to run out. **Pressure** builds up inside the volcano and causes an explosive eruption. Explosive eruptions can be dangerous. Showers of rock as well as tiny **particles** of ash blast into the air. The blast can knock down trees for miles. Explosive volcanoes can cause avalanches and produce swift rivers of flowing mud. Clouds of gases and ash can form. This air **pollution** can make it hard for people to breathe. It can also clog airplane engines. Volcanic particles can even cause Earth's temperature to cool.

VOCABULARY

Read these words from the passage. Check the words you know.

- [ ] erupt
- [ ] landforms
- [ ] particles
- [ ] pollution
- [ ] pressure
- [ ] vents

Functional Vocabulary

- [ ] classify

2. Vocabulary Focus

Write each word from the vocabulary list next to its definition.

_____ 1. small pieces of something

_____ 2. to put things into groups based on how they are alike

_____ 3. introduction into the environment of substances that make air, water, or soil dirty and unsafe

_____ 4. to send out lava, rocks, and ash

_____ 5. holes through which gases or liquids can escape

_____ 6. the force that is produced when things press or push against one another

_____ 7. natural features found on Earth's surface

© New Readers Press. All rights reserved.

3. Work With New Vocabulary

Complete each idea. Write your answer on the line.

1. You know that a volcano has **erupted** when _____

   _____

2. Some examples of **landforms** include _____

   _____

3. You can tell that there is **pollution** when _____

   _____

4. To **classify** the cars in a parking lot, you could _____

   _____

5. If you wanted to **compress** an empty can, you could _____

   _____

6. When a volcano erupts, you can tell where the **vents** are because _____

   _____

7. You can tell that an explosive volcano has a lot of **pressure** inside it because _____

   _____

Answer the questions. Explain your answers.

In the word *glacier*, the letters *ci* make the *sh* sound in *shop*.

8. Can you see a **glacier** move? Explain your answer.

   _____

9. Describe a change that is **gradual**.

   _____

10. Would it be easy to count the **particles** that are released when a volcano erupts? Explain your answer.

    _____

11. How might living at a high **elevation** be different from living at sea level?

    _____

12. Name a **dense** object. How do you know that it's dense?

    _____

13. What happens when a beach **erodes**?

    _____

14. Describe something you have **created**. Why did you create it?

    _____

© New Readers Press. All rights reserved.

4. Prefix ex–

The prefix *ex–* means "out of; from." For example, if you *exhale*, you breathe out.

Match each word to its definition. Write the letter of the correct definition on the line.

_____	1. excavate	a. the outer part of something
_____	2. exclude	b. to burst in a violent away and force parts outward
_____	3. explode	c. to send products out of the country
_____	4. export	d. no longer active (in the case of a volcano)
_____	5. exterior	e. to keep something out
_____	6. extinct	f. to dig something out of the ground

> Another meaning of the prefix *ex–* is "former," as in *ex-roommate*, *ex-wife*. When *ex–* means "former," the prefix is followed by a hyphen.

5. Suffix –ive

When the suffix *–ive* occurs at the end of an adjective, it means "tending toward" or "having the nature of." For example, the word *active* means "characterized by action."

Read the definition of each word with the suffix –ive. Then use the word in a sentence about glaciers or volcanoes.

1. **abrasive**: rough; causing damage by rubbing

_____

2. **destructive**: causing a lot of harm

_____

3. **massive**: large and heavy

_____

4. **explosive**: able to explode or blow up

_____

5. **extensive**: covering a large area

_____

6. **inactive**: not active; not able to erupt

_____

> Look for familiar roots or similar words to figure out word meanings. Use what you know about *explode*, *destroy*, and *mass* to figure out *explosive*, *destructive*, and *massive*.

© New Readers Press. All rights reserved.

6. Context Clues: Definitions, Explanations, and General Clues

Clue words like *means*, *meaning*, *is defined as*, and *refers to* can help you find definitions or explanations as you read.

Scientific or technical texts often have definitions or explanations of words. Look for definitions of important concepts as you read.

Read the passage. Look for clues to the meaning of each boldfaced word. Then complete the sentences.

It may not seem like it, but Earth is **continually** changing. Some changes are **rapid** and visible. Lava erupting from a volcano is an example. But other changes are not so **obvious**. They happen much more slowly. An example of this is **weathering**. Weathering is the process by which rock on Earth's surface is worn away and broken into smaller pieces. Erosion helps move these small pieces of rock to other places. The material that is **removed** from one place and deposited in another is called **sediment**.

There are many ways for weathering to occur. Water can get inside cracks in a rock. When that water freezes, it expands. The ice acts like a **wedge** pushing against the sides of the crack and making it larger. **Abrasion** is another kind of weathering. Abrasion occurs when materials rub or grind against one another. For example, river rocks become smooth because they are always bumping together. The bumping and scraping wears away any **rough** edges and points. Even animals can cause weathering. Animals that **burrow**, or dig tunnels in the ground, move soil around and expose new surfaces.

1. **Continually** means _____

2. Something that is **rapid** is _____

3. Something that is **obvious** is _____

4. **Weathering** is _____

5. If something is **removed**, it is _____

6. **Sediment** is _____

7. A **wedge** is _____

8. **Abrasion** is _____

9. If something is **rough**, it _____

10. When animals **burrow**, they _____

© New Readers Press. All rights reserved.

7. Parts of Speech and the Dictionary

Many words can be either nouns or verbs. Check how the word is used in the sentence to figure out what part of speech it is playing.

On the short line, write the part of speech of each boldfaced word. Then look the word up in the dictionary and write the definition that matches how the word is used in the sentence.

Figure out the part of speech before you look a word up in the dictionary. This will help you find the right dictionary entry.

1. The **flow** of mountain streams carries sediment from the mountains to valleys below.

   _____ _____

2. Pebbles and stones carried by glaciers can **scratch** rocks and leave grooves in them.

   _____ _____

3. When erosion occurs, rock and soil are carried from their **original** location and deposited somewhere else.

   _____ _____

4. Glaciers **store** much of the world's freshwater supply.

   _____ _____

5. When rocks continually rub together, any sharp **points** get worn away.

   _____ _____

8. Multiple-Meaning Words

You can use context to figure out the correct meaning of many words with multiple meanings. If you still aren't sure of a word's meaning, look it up in the dictionary.

Look at each underlined word. Circle the letter of the best definition.

If you are trying to choose from multiple definitions of a word, try substituting the different definitions into the sentence. Think about which definition makes the most sense.

1. Lambert Glacier in Antarctica is a large <u>sheet</u> of ice about 60 miles wide and 260 miles long.
   a. a piece of cloth that covers something
   b. a wide flat surface

2. An underwater volcano can create a <u>chain</u> of islands. The Hawaiian Islands are one example.
   a. a group of things that are connected
   b. a series of metal links that are joined

3. Volcanoes produce different kinds of rock depending on what is in the lava. Some rocks are rough and grainy. Other volcanic rocks are <u>smooth</u> like glass.
   a. happening without sudden starts and stops
   b. flat and even without rough spots

4. When glaciers move downhill, they grind away at rock and <u>carve</u> U-shaped valleys.
   a. to make a piece of art by cutting away material
   b. to make something by cutting into a surface

5. Glaciers usually move downhill faster when the <u>slope</u> is steep.
   a. the downward slant of an area of land
   b. an area covered by snow that people ski down

© New Readers Press. All rights reserved.

Unit 9 Review

Circle the letter of the answer that best completes each sentence.

1. A **glacier** is made of _____.

   a. ice
   b. rock
   c. lava

2. If you were going to **excavate** a piece of land, you would use a _____.

   a. pencil
   b. camera
   c. shovel

3. You would be most likely to see **pollution** _____.

   a. on the top of a tall icy mountain
   b. in a large city with many cars and factories
   c. on a small chain of islands in the middle of the ocean

4. **Abrasion** occurs when _____.

   a. animals dig holes in the soil
   b. lava flows from a volcano
   c. rocks grind together

Choose the best word to complete each sentence. Write it on the line.

5. An _____ eruption of a volcano can be dangerous. Rock, ash, and gases can shoot miles into the air.

   abrasive   **explosive**   **original**

6. Glaciers _____ a lot of water. In some parts of the world, melting glaciers provide drinking water.

   export   **remove**   **store**

7. Rocks in creeks and rivers bump into each other. Over long periods of time, the surfaces of these rocks become _____.

   obvious   **dense**   **smooth**

8. Glaciers form in cold areas where there is snow year-round. Over time, new layers of snow _____ older layers of snow into a dense mass of ice.

   compress   **carve**   **classify**

9. The process of weathering breaks rocks down into smaller pieces. This _____ is then carried by water, wind, or ice and deposited somewhere else.

   landform   **wedge**   **sediment**

What forces have changed the surface of Earth over time? What have these forces done to the surface? Write your answer on a separate sheet of paper. Use at least five words you learned in this unit. Circle the vocabulary words you use.

© New Readers Press. All rights reserved.

TESTING TIP:

Being an active reader can help you as you take a test. As you read passages, write notes in the margins about important ideas. Highlight or underline key terms. This can help you understand what you have read and find information when you answer questions. You can make notes beside the test questions, too. Circle any important words in the questions. *(Note: first make sure it is OK to write on a paper version of a test or to take notes on a computer.)*

Circle the letter of the best answer.

1. **Which meaning of *dense* matches how the word is used in this passage?**

   Glaciers form when snow falls. The new snow presses down on older layers. The snow becomes a <u>dense</u> sheet of ice.

   A not very smart

   B hard to see through

   C having parts that are pushed very close together

   D containing a lot of difficult information

2. **Which word best completes the passage?**

   The movement of a typical glacier is _____. It might move only about a foot per day.

   A explosive

   B gradual

   C massive

   D rapid

3. **What happens when something *explodes*?**

   A It carries material from one place to another.

   B It flows down a mountain or slope.

   C It slowly wears away.

   D It shoots pieces out in a violent way.

4. **What does the word *massive* mean in this passage?**

   A <u>massive</u> glacier in Greenland is nearly two miles thick. The weight of the ice has compressed the land beneath it so much that the land is now below sea level.

   A very smooth and shiny

   B thick and cloudy

   C thin and runny

   D very large and heavy

5. **What does *particles* mean in this sentence?**

   When some volcanoes erupt, they blast <u>particles</u> of rock and ash into the air.

   A bits of ice

   B large boulders

   C small pieces

   D hot liquids

6. **Which word best completes the passage?**

   The Appalachian Mountains in the eastern U.S. were once 30,000 feet tall. Today, because of the process of _____, they are less than 7,000 feet tall.

   A weathering

   B pollution

   C sediment

   D elevation

Check your answers on page 107.

© New Readers Press. All rights reserved.

10 Natural Disasters

© New Readers Press. All rights reserved.

VOCABULARY

Read these words from the passage. Check the words you know.

- [ ] destroy
- [ ] embers
- [ ] flammable
- [ ] fuel
- [ ] humidity
- [ ] wildfires

Functional Vocabulary

- [ ] occur

Wildfires

Fire requires **fuel**, heat, and oxygen. If you remove any part of the "fire triangle," there is no fire.

According to the U.S. Forest Service, an average of more than 73,000 **wildfires** burn about 7.3 million acres of private, state, and federal land and more than 2,600 structures in the United States every year. Ninety percent of those wildfires are caused by human activities such as burning yard waste, improperly putting out campfires, tossing lit cigarettes, and deliberately starting fires. The remaining 10 percent of wildfires **occur** as a result of weather events. A lightning strike during a drought, for example, when plants are dried out and more **flammable** than usual, can easily start a fire.

A small fire turns into a wildfire when there is plenty of fuel (dead leaves, grass, and fallen branches), low **humidity** or precipitation, high temperature, and high winds. Winds can carry burning **embers** to other fuel sources, starting additional fires. Wildfires can move very quickly, up to 14 miles an hour.

Although wildfires **destroy** property and habitats, they also create necessary change. They are an important part of the cycle in most ecosystems. For example, some forest fires allow trees to produce seeds or clear the ground for new plants, trees, and wildlife.

1. Vocabulary Focus

Write each word from the vocabulary list beside its definition.

_____ 1. uncontrolled fires, usually in wild land areas

_____ 2. anything that can burn

_____ 3. moisture in the atmosphere

_____ 4. cause something to no longer exist

_____ 5. small glowing pieces of wood or coal from a fire

_____ 6. to happen

_____ 7. burns easily

Hurricanes

Hurricanes are giant storms. They cause damage to property as well as loss of human life.

Hurricanes are the most powerful storms on Earth. They form over warm tropical oceans with temperatures of at least 80°F. As a storm grows, winds begin to **rotate** around the calm center, or eye, of the storm. Hurricanes can grow to several hundred miles in diameter. They are so large that they are easily visible from space.

Scientists **categorize** hurricanes by wind speed on a **scale** of 1 to 5. Knowing a storm's category lets experts estimate how much property damage a hurricane's winds will cause. A Category 1 storm has winds of 74 to 95 miles per hour. A Category 5, the most severe storm, has winds of more than 157 miles per hour. Hurricane winds can cause buildings to **collapse** and trees and power lines to fall.

Strong winds are only one kind of danger. Hurricanes also produce **storm surges** when they **approach** land. The rise in ocean level can be up to 30 feet. A storm surge is very dangerous for **coastal** areas. The water can wash away beaches, roads, and houses near the shore. As hurricanes move over land, they produce bands of heavy rain and strong winds. Some areas can get up to two feet or more of rain. The intense rainfall can cause flooding even in inland areas.

VOCABULARY

Read these words from the passage. Check the words you know.

- ☐ approach
- ☐ coastal
- ☐ collapse
- ☐ rotate
- ☐ scale
- ☐ storm surges

Functional Vocabulary

- ☐ categorize

2. Vocabulary Focus

Complete each sentence with a word from the vocabulary list.

1. When you _____ something, you move towards it.

2. When buildings _____, they fall down suddenly.

3. Rapid rises in sea level caused by hurricanes are _____.

4. A range of numbers used to show the strength or size of something is a
   _____.

5. A _____ area is land that borders an ocean.

6. When you _____ something, you put it into a group according to the type of things it is.

7. When objects _____, they spin or turn in a circle.

© New Readers Press. All rights reserved.

3. Work With New Vocabulary

Write T *if a statement is true. Write* F *if the statement is false, and then explain why it is false.*

1. _____ Burning trees are kinds of **embers**.

   _____

2. _____ **Storm surges** mostly affect **coastal** areas.

   _____

3. _____ **Wildfires** need **fuel**, heat, and wind to get started.

   _____

4. _____ Wildfires **destroy** millions of acres of land a year. They are dangerous and completely bad for wildlife and wild lands.

   _____

5. _____ Hurricanes don't cause damage after they **approach** land.

   _____

6. _____ It is safe to leave **flammable** materials near an open fire.

   _____

Answer the questions. Explain your answers.

7. What is something in your home that you could measure on a **scale** from 1 to 5? How would you define a Category 1 and a Category 5?

   _____

8. Hurricane winds rotate. What are two other things that **rotate**?

   _____

9. How do you feel when there's a lot of **humidity** in the air?

   _____

10. Name three things you **categorize** at work, at home, or at school.

    _____

11. What kind of natural disasters **occur** in your part of the United States?

    _____

12. What would you do if you saw a building that was about to **collapse**?

    _____

© New Readers Press. All rights reserved.

4. Roots *vid, vis*

The roots *vid* and *vis* mean "to see" or "to look at." For example, *vision* means "the ability to see."

Read the definition of each word with the root vis *or* vid. *Then use the word in a sentence.*

1. **evidence**: facts that prove that something is true

   _____

2. **visible**: able to be seen

   _____

3. **revise**: to make a change or correction to something

   _____

4. **envision**: to picture something in your mind

   _____

5. **advise**: to suggest or recommend something that should be done

   _____

6. **provide**: to supply or give something that is needed

   _____

5. Suffix *–ity*

The suffix *–ity* means "the state of being something." The suffix *–ity* forms a noun from an adjective. For example, when meteorologists talk about the *humidity* in the air, they are talking about how humid the air is.

The final *e* is dropped when the suffix *–ity* is added.

Choose a word from the list to complete each sentence. If you aren't sure of a word's meaning, look it up in the dictionary.

ability	activity	majority	probability	similarity

1. If there's a high _____ of rain, it's very likely that it's going to rain.

2. There is very little _____ in the eye of a hurricane.

3. Hurricanes have the _____ to destroy entire communities.

4. Is there any _____ between ice and rain?

5. The _____ of hurricanes occur between June and November.

Add the suffix –ity to each word below. Then write a definition of the new word.

6. equal: _____   _____

7. secure: _____   _____

© New Readers Press. All rights reserved.

6. Context Clues: General Clues, Definitions, and Examples

Before you read a passage, think about the topic. Ask yourself what kinds of words you expect to find. Then look for clues, definitions, and examples that support your answers.

Read this passage about ice storms. Look for and underline any clues that help you figure out the meanings of boldfaced words. Write the meanings of the lines.

An ice storm is a winter storm with freezing rain. The U.S. National Weather Service defines an ice storm as a storm in which at least 0.25 of an inch of ice **accumulates**, or piles up gradually over time.

An ice storm begins when snowflakes fall through a warm layer in the atmosphere and melt into rain. The raindrops then move into a thin layer of very cold air near the ground. This causes them to freeze on contact with **exposed**, or unprotected, surfaces. If the rain freezes before it touches the ground, it becomes **sleet** rather than ice.

Ice storms cover everything in a clear **glaze** of frozen rain. The weight of the ice can split trees in half and the **severe** cold can turn roads into solid sheets of ice.

1. To **accumulate** means to _____

2. To be **exposed** means to be _____

3. **Sleet** is _____

4. A **glaze** is _____

5. If something is **severe**, it is _____

Words and phrases such as *when, in other words,* and *in some cases* are clues that a writer is giving examples or definitions.

Sometimes you can understand the meaning of an unfamiliar word by finding words or clues that are examples or definitions of the word.

Underline any examples that help explain the boldfaced words. Then write definitions. Check your answers in a dictionary.

6. Just a quarter inch of ice can cause serious power **outages**. In some cases, people have gone without power for weeks.

   definition: _____

7. As freezing rain falls, it **encases** everything it touches in ice. If your car is completely covered, you may have to wait for days before you can even open the door.

   definition: _____

8. For freezing rain to occur there must be close to 100% humidity. In other words, the air needs to be completely filled with **moisture**.

   definition: _____

9. Even a quarter inch of ice can create very dangerous and **hazardous** conditions.

   definition: _____

© New Readers Press. All rights reserved.

7. Parts of Speech and the Dictionary

Words can play more than one part in speech. Try to figure out what part of speech a word is playing before you look it up in the dictionary.

On the short line, write the part of speech of each boldfaced word. Then look up the word in the dictionary and write the definition that matches how the word is used in the sentence.

If a word names a person, place, thing, or idea, it is a noun.

1. Burning dead wood and fuel before fire season can help **control** fires in some forests.

   _____   _____

2. Since the 1850s, the U.S. has had an **average** of six hurricanes per year.

   _____   _____

3. Wildfires can spread at a **rate** of about 14 miles an hour.

   _____   _____

4. The eye of a hurricane is **calm** and free of clouds.

   _____   _____

5. When too much ice **covers** power lines, the lines can break and fall.

   _____   _____

8. Multiple-Meaning Words

Many words have more than one meaning. Think about the topic you are reading about. The topic can provide clues about the correct meaning.

Look at each underlined word. Circle the letter of the best definition.

1. Some wildfires burn brush growing near the <u>ground</u>, while others burn the tops of trees.
   a. the surface of the earth
   b. broken up into small pieces

2. <u>Bands</u> of rain and thunderstorms can move across an area after a hurricane hits land.
   a. thick lines
   b. flat, thin strips or loops of material to put around something

3. The U.S. Forest Service offers tips that owners of <u>private</u> land can use to protect property from fire.
   a. personal or secret
   b. owned by individuals, not by the government

4. After a winter storm, roads can be <u>solid</u> sheets of ice.
   a. strong and well made
   b. hard or firm

5. A wildfire can <u>renew</u> the soil by adding nutrients.
   a. to continue for an additional period of time
   b. to make something fresh or strong again

© New Readers Press. All rights reserved.

Unit 10 Review

Complete each sentence with a word from the list.

approaches	categorize	glaze	moisture	occur	renew

1. Ice storms in the United States _____ most often during December and January.

2. Scientists _____ hurricanes by their strength so that people can prepare for the storms.

3. When a hurricane _____ land, it can push a mound of water ashore. This can cause serious flooding.

4. Fuels with a lot of _____ are harder to burn than fuels that are dry.

5. Wildfires can help some ecosystems. They _____ the soil and make it ready for new plants to grow.

6. In an ice storm, a _____ covers plants and power lines. The ice is heavy, which can cause tree limbs to break and power lines to fall.

Choose the best word to finish each sentence. Write it on the line.

7. Firefighters do not know with _____ which way a wildfire will burn. They have to be ready in case a fire changes direction.

   activity   **certainty**   **majority**

8. A storm surge is dangerous because water can _____ roads and flood buildings in coastal areas.

   expose   **control**   **cover**

9. Ice storms and hurricanes are examples of _____ weather.

   calm   **severe**   **solid**

10. After firefighters put out a fire, they look for _____ or proof of what caused it.

   evidence   **similarity**   **ability**

How are people affected by natural disasters like wildfires and hurricanes? Write your answer on a separate sheet of paper. Use at least five words you learned in this unit. Circle the vocabulary words you use.

© New Readers Press. All rights reserved.

TESTING TIP:

Sometimes a test question will ask you to choose the *best answer* or ask which answer choice *best matches* a word's meaning. When you see the word *best* in a question, it means you must pick the answer that is most correct. Make sure you read all the answer choices carefully before choosing one, since some choices might be partly correct.

Circle the letter of the best answer.

1. **Which meaning of *scale* best matches how the word is used in this sentence?**

   Hurricanes are ranked on a <u>scale</u> of 1 to 5 based on their wind speed.

   A a tool for weighing people or things

   B the small pieces of skin on the body of a fish

   C a system of numbers used to measure something

   D the size or level of something

2. **Which word best completes the sentence?**

   In an ice storm, at least 0.25 inch of ice _____, or builds up, on surfaces.

   A accumulates

   B encases

   C collapses

   D approaches

3. **Which of the following is an example of something that could *collapse*?**

   A a storm surge

   B a building

   C moisture

   D a pencil

4. **What does it mean if something is *visible*?**

   A It causes damage.

   B It freezes easily.

   C It can be burned.

   D It can be seen.

5. **What does *fuel* mean in this sentence?**

   All wildfires need <u>fuel</u>, heat, and oxygen.

   A strong winds

   B something to burn

   C a wide-open area

   D warm temperatures

6. **What word in the passage means about the same as *rotates*?**

   A hurricane is a large storm that <u>rotates</u> around an eye. Hurricanes begin as groups of thunderstorms that form over warm water. Hurricanes that affect the United States spin in a counter-clockwise direction.

   A begin

   B form

   C affect

   D spin

Check your answers on page 107.

© New Readers Press. All rights reserved.

11 Climate Cycles and Change

VOCABULARY

Read these words from the passage. Check the words you know.

- ☐ atmosphere
- ☐ cycles
- ☐ data
- ☐ direct
- ☐ meteorologists
- ☐ varies

Functional Vocabulary

- ☐ predict

Weather, Climate, and Climate Change

It is normal for the weather to change from one hour to another or one day to another. But when a pattern changes over many years, it's called "climate change."

Earth's **atmosphere** is made up of gases that keep the planet warm and protect us from the **direct** rays of the Sun.

Weather is a mix of two things: the state of the atmosphere at a specific place and time and the way this atmosphere affects life on Earth. **Meteorologists** record and **predict** weather events, including temperatures, sunshine and cloudiness, winds, flooding, and storms.

If you collect weather **data** in a particular place and average it over a long period of time you will see overall patterns. These patterns identify the climate of the place. Climate **varies** around the world and is affected by things like amount of sunlight and altitude.

Like the weather, climate is always changing. Long-term average temperatures may go up or down. A weather pattern can change. Some changes are natural. Others are caused by humans. Most scientists agree that the warming we are currently experiencing is due to human activity as well as natural **cycles** of cooling and warming.

1. Vocabulary Focus

Write the word from the list that means the same thing as the underlined words.

_____ 1. People disagree about whether recent changes to weather <u>series of events that repeat</u> are natural or man-made.

_____ 2. Airlines work with <u>scientists who predict the weather</u> so pilots know what to expect when they take off, fly, and land.

_____ 3. Weather is the condition of the <u>mixture of gases that surround Earth</u> at a particular time and place.

_____ 4. Scientists study weather and temperature <u>facts or information</u> in order to understand climate change

_____ 5. The definition of "perfect weather" <u>is different</u> from person to person.

_____ 6. Thomas Jefferson started to <u>say what will happen based on science and observation</u> the weather in the late 1700s.

_____ 7. Life could not exist on Earth if the atmosphere didn't protect us from the <u>coming straight from the source</u> rays of the Sun.

© New Readers Press. All rights reserved.

El Niño and La Niña

Sometimes changes in climate have natural causes. El Niño and La Niña are part of a climate cycle that repeats every two to seven years.

El Niño is an "ocean **phenomenon**," a **mass** of warm ocean water that develops in the Equatorial Pacific Ocean and moves east. As the water becomes warmer, ocean conditions and sea life are affected.

The heated water warms the air above, which affects atmospheric **circulation**, the movement of air around the globe. El Niño affects weather patterns in places such as Indonesia, Africa, and the Americas. In the U.S., the **impact** of El Niño is usually felt during the winter. In the Northwest and Alaska, weather is likely to be more **mild** and dry. In the South, conditions are likely to be cooler and wetter than usual during an El Niño winter. Extreme weather events like hurricanes, floods, and droughts are more likely in an El Niño year.

While El Niño is a large area of extra-warm ocean surface temperatures, La Niña is the **reverse**. La Niña is a **sustained** cooling of the same surface waters and atmosphere in the Pacific. During a La Niña year, winter temperatures are warmer than normal in the Southeast U.S. and cooler than normal in the Northwest. El Niño usually lasts nine to 12 months; La Niña can stay around for two years or more.

2. Vocabulary Focus

Complete each sentence with a word from the vocabulary list.

1. If something continues for a long period, it is _____.

2. The _____ is the complete opposite of something.

3. A weather event like a rainstorm that is not very strong is _____.

4. A _____ is something that happens and can be observed, but is not well understood.

5. The effect something has on something else is its _____.

6. _____ is the movement of water, air, etc. around something.

7. A large amount of something without a clear shape is a _____.

VOCABULARY

Read these words from the passage. Check the words you know.

☐ circulation

☐ mass

☐ mild

☐ phenomenon

☐ reverse

☐ sustained

Functional Vocabulary

☐ impact

© New Readers Press. All rights reserved.

3. Work With New Vocabulary

Answer the questions. Explain your answers.

1. If you have a **mild** temperature, do you go about things as usual, go to the doctor, or stay home?

_____

2. Name three things **meteorologists** report on.

_____

3. What is the **impact** of too much rain in a desert? In a forest? In a city?

_____

4. Meteorologists **predict** what the weather will be like in the future. What other people predict the future as part of their work?

_____

The word *data* is plural in form but is used with both plural and singular verbs.

5. What **data** about the weather would you want to know if you were going to the beach or the movies? Where would you look for that data?

_____

6. What have you worked on for a **sustained** period of time? Why did it take so long?

_____

7. The atmosphere provides the oxygen we breathe and protects us from the **direct** rays of the Sun. What do you think Earth would be like if we had no atmosphere?

_____

Write T *if a statement is true. Write* F *if the statement is false and explain why it is false.*

8. _____ If something is the **reverse** of hot, it is very hot.

_____

9. _____ Our **atmosphere** is the mix of gases inside Earth.

_____

The plural of *phenomenon* is *phenomena*.

10. _____ Scientists understand what causes most natural **phenomena**.

_____

11. _____ Events that happen once and never again are said to happen in **cycles**.

_____

12. _____ When something **varies**, it changes.

_____

13. _____ A square is an example of a **mass**.

_____

14. _____ Something in **circulation** stays in one place.

_____

© New Readers Press. All rights reserved.

4. Prefixes *circ-*, *circum-*

The prefixes *circ-* and *circum-* mean "around, about." You know, for example, that a circle is a round shape with no beginning or end.

Match each word to its definition. Write the letter of the correct definition on the line.

_____ 1. circuit

_____ 2. circus

_____ 3. circumstances

_____ 4. circulate

_____ 5. circular

_____ 6. circumference

a. to move around freely, returning to the starting point

b. the facts around a particular situation

c. a route or a path around something

d. a group of traveling entertainers, often in a large tent

e. the length of a line around the edge of a circle

f. in the shape of a circle

> The large circle in which a *circus* performs is the *ring*. Do you see the connection between *circus* and *around*?

5. Suffix *-ic*

The suffix *-ic* means "nature of, like." When you add this suffix to a noun or verb, it usually creates an adjective, as in *atmospheric* (*atmosphere* + *-ic*).

Complete each sentence with a word from the list; then define the word. If you aren't sure of a word's meaning, look it up in the dictionary.

> To form adverbs from adjectives ending in *-ic*, add *-ally* (*economically*) and sometimes *-ly* (*publicly*).

academic	economic	problematic	public	specific	volcanic

1. Weather is a clearly defined and _____ event or condition that happens over hours or days.

   definition: _____

2. Clouds, _____ eruptions, oceans, and people all affect the climate.

   definition: _____

3. Climate change is a _____ concern; it impacts everyone.

   definition: _____

4. Dealing with climate change is _____. What makes it so difficult?

   definition: _____

5. Climate change has _____ impacts on countries around the world. Every year, millions of dollars are spent fighting its effects.

   definition: _____

6. Climate change is an _____ subject at some universities.

   definition: _____

© New Readers Press. All rights reserved.

6. Context Clues: General Clues and Synonyms

Don't just memorize the definitions of vocabulary words. Be sure you understand what the definitions mean. Tests and dictionaries do not always define things the same way.

When you can't understand a sentence because of an unfamiliar word, check for synonyms. If you find a synonym that you know, reread the sentence with that new word. It should make sense.

Read the passage. Look for clues and synonyms to help you understand the meaning of each boldfaced word. Write the meaning on the line.

Earth's climate has changed many times over millions of years. Scientists study **global** climate change because it affects every living thing on Earth.

Climate changes before the mid-18th century and the Industrial Revolution were due to natural causes, such as volcanic eruptions. But **recent**, not long ago, climate change cannot be explained by natural causes alone. The climate is changing faster than it has in the past. Human activities have **contributed** to climate change by adding carbon dioxide and other gases to the atmosphere. In fact, human activities **emit** more than 135 times as much carbon dioxide as volcanoes send out each year.

Carbon dioxide is the primary contributor to climate change. Human activities like burning **fossil fuels** (coal, oil, and natural gas) release large amounts of carbon dioxide.

1. **Global** means _____

2. **Recent** means _____

3. To **contribute** means _____

4. To **emit** means to _____

5. **Fossil fuels** are _____

Context clues can be found when the unknown word is defined in the sentence. They are usually set off by commas.

Underline any clues or synonyms that help explain the boldfaced words. Then write a definition for each word. Check your answers in a dictionary.

6. The climate is changing more **rapidly**, or more quickly, than it has in the past. Scientists are concerned about this change in speed.

   definition: _____

7. Human activities release large **quantities** of carbon dioxide into the atmosphere. The amount is estimated to be more than 30 billion tons every year.

   definition: _____

The opposite of *renewable* is *nonrenewable*.

8. If we want to slow climate change, we need to make use of **renewable** energy resources, such as the Sun and wind. Energy from these sources can be replaced naturally.

   definition: _____

9. One possible result of climate change is that **extreme** weather, like large storms and long heat waves, will become increasingly common.

   definition: _____

© New Readers Press. All rights reserved.

7. Parts of Speech and the Dictionary

Identifying a multiple-meaning word's part of speech can help you determine what the word means in a particular sentence. Choose the part of speech that makes sense in context by looking at words that surround the unknown word.

Circle the part of speech of each boldfaced word. Then look up the word in a dictionary. Write the definition that matches how the word is used in the sentence.

Guessing the meaning of an unknown word is useful when you understand the words around it. But if you can't guess a word, look it up.

noun   verb   1. Atmospheric scientists **link** only a few extreme weather events to El Niño.

_____

noun   verb   2. Earth's atmosphere is divided into four **layers**.

_____

noun   adjective   3. When El Niño weakens during the spring, it moves into its **neutral** stage.

_____

noun   verb   4. Before humans, the only **factors** causing climate change were natural.

_____

noun   verb   5. Earth's temperature depends on the **balance** between the energy entering and the energy leaving the planet.

_____

8. Multiple-Meaning Words

Understanding multiple meaning words is important for studying many academic subjects, especially science. As you come across a word with more than one meaning, keep the overall scientific context in mind.

Look at each underlined word. Circle the letter of the best definition.

1. To what <u>degree</u> do you believe climate change is a serious problem?
   a. a measurement in temperature
   b. an amount of something

2. As the ocean warms, fish may lose a <u>major</u> source of their food.
   a. more important, bigger, or more serious than others of the same type
   b. a mid-level officer in the armed forces

3. It's <u>critical</u> that all of us use our power to slow down climate change.
   a. expressing a negative opinion
   b. very important

4. A meteorologist <u>forecasts</u> the weather using data from various sources, such as weather stations and NASA.
   a. what someone thinks will happen in the future
   b. predicts a future event

5. Scientists have recorded Earth's climate, <u>dating</u> back millions of years.
   a. writing the date on
   b. starting from

© New Readers Press. All rights reserved.

Unit 11 Review

Choose the best word to finish each sentence. Write it on the line.

1. The _____ impact of global climate change includes damage to property, lost work days, and an increase in healthcare costs.

    economic   **academic**   **volcanic**

2. If the temperature is going to be much higher or lower than usual, meteorologists forecast _____ weather.

    extreme   **neutral**   **mild**

3. _____ rain causes flooding.

    Circular   **Specific**   **Sustained**

4. Air _____ around Earth and distributes heat.

    dates   **reverses**   **circulates**

5. Scientists use _____ from many sources to better understand climate change.

    data   **circulation**   **factors**

Circle the letter of the answer that best completes each sentence.

6. **Fossil fuels** _____.
    a. are millions of years old
    b. help predict the weather
    c. come from the atmosphere

7. The **impact** of something is _____.
    a. how strong it is
    b. the effect it has
    c. what it's like inside

8. The **circumference** of Earth is the _____ the planet.
    a. distance around
    b. round shape of
    c. movement around

9. When the weather **varies** from day to day, it _____.
    a. changes
    b. circulates
    c. balances

How can weather and climate change affect your life? Write your answer on a separate sheet of paper. Use at least five words you learned in this unit. Circle the vocabulary words you use.

© New Readers Press. All rights reserved.

TESTING TIP:

When you're taking a multiple-choice test, cover up the answer options with a piece of paper or with your hand while you read the question. Try to come up with your own answer before choosing an option. If you see your answer on the page, circle it, and check that it is the best option.

Circle the letter of the best answer.

1. **What does the word *direct* mean in this sentence?**

   The atmosphere protects us from the <u>direct</u> rays of the Sun.

   A said or done in a clear and honest way

   B connected to something in a clear way

   C with nothing in the way

   D the exact words

2. **Which meaning of *balance* matches how the word is used in this sentence?**

   For global temperatures to be regular, Earth's energy to and from the Sun has to be in <u>balance</u>.

   A a steady position without falling

   B fair and just

   C when two things are equal

   D the amount of something left over

3. **Which word best completes the sentence?**

   Gasses that our vehicles (planes, trains, cars, etc.) _____ into the atmosphere are one cause of climate change.

   A predict

   B emit

   C vary

   D link

4. **Choose the best word to complete the passage.**

   In 2015, every state in the country had an above-average annual temperature. The annual temperature for the United States that year was 2.4 _____ F above the 20th century average. It was the second warmest year on record.

   A links

   B degrees

   C cycles

   D factors

5. **Which word or words in the passage mean about the same as *precipitation*?**

   Climate is defined by average <u>precipitation</u> and temperature and by extreme weather events such as storms and floods. Total annual rain and snow have increased in the United States.

   A temperature

   B weather event

   C storms and floods

   D rain and snow

6. **What does the word *critical* mean in this passage?**

   Do you want to limit climate change? Then it's <u>critical</u> that you take time to think about changes you can make in your own life.

   A extremely important

   B serious and possibly dangerous

   C showing disapproval

   D judging something or someone as good or bad

Check your answers beginning on page 107.

© New Readers Press. All rights reserved.

VOCABULARY

Read these words from the passage. Check the words you know.

- ☐ astronomers
- ☐ constellations
- ☐ galaxies
- ☐ magnify
- ☐ orbit
- ☐ revolve

Functional Vocabulary

- ☐ confirm

Observing Space

"Man must rise above the Earth—to the top of the atmosphere and beyond—for only [then] will he fully understand the world in which he lives." –Socrates, Greek philosopher

Humans have long observed objects in the sky. The earliest **astronomers** looked for groups of stars in the night sky. They named these **constellations** for objects, animals, and characters that they resembled. People used the constellations as a kind of calendar to know when to plant and harvest crops. Constellations also helped with navigation across oceans and deserts. People used the positions of the stars to guide them.

In 1609, Galileo developed a telescope that could **magnify** objects by 20 times. The telescope let Galileo see details on the moon and discover four of Jupiter's moons. His observations helped prove that planets **revolve** around the Sun, not Earth.

Over time, telescopes became larger and more powerful. In the 1920s, Edwin Hubble used a telescope to **confirm** that the universe had **galaxies** beyond our own. In 1990, a telescope named after Hubble was launched into Earth's **orbit**. Because the Hubble Space Telescope is above Earth's atmosphere, it has a much better view of the universe than telescopes on Earth. The telescope has made more than a million observations and traveled more than 3 billion miles. The data it has sent has transformed what we know about the universe.

1. Vocabulary Focus

Complete each sentence with a word from the vocabulary list.

1. When you _____ something, you prove that it is true or correct.

2. When you _____ something, you make it look bigger than it really is.

3. Scientists who study the stars and planets are _____.

4. The curved or circular path an object follows around a planet or sun is its _____.

5. _____ are large groups or systems of stars in space.

6. To _____ means to move in a circle around something.

7. Groups of stars that form patterns are called _____.

© New Readers Press. All rights reserved.

Impact Earth

A number of science fiction movies show Earth being destroyed by objects from space. Is Earth really at risk?

Our planet has been hit by objects from space for as long as it has existed. Every day, pieces of **debris**, most the size of grains of sand or pebbles, hit Earth's atmosphere. In fact, more than 100 tons of dust and particles hit Earth daily. Many of these objects burn up when they reach Earth's atmosphere, making a flash of light as they move. People call these flashes of light "shooting stars," even though they are not stars at all.

Larger pieces of matter, such as asteroids or parts of **comets**, can also **collide** with Earth. A piece of rock or metal that survives the trip through the atmosphere to land on Earth is called a **meteorite**. Small meteorites usually go unnoticed unless they hit something like a car or a house. However, objects larger than a few hundred feet can form **craters** on Earth and greatly impact the planet. One example is the asteroid that formed the Chicxulub crater in Mexico. The asteroid was likely 6 miles across, and it made a crater 110 miles wide. Its impact caused the extinction of dinosaurs and other species millions of years ago.

Today scientists with NASA, America's space agency, **monitor** our **solar system** for objects that could collide with Earth. NASA tracks asteroids and comets and calculates their pathways. If Earth is in danger, we should have plenty of notice.

2. Vocabulary Focus

Write a word from the vocabulary list next to its definition.

_____ 1. a piece of rock or metal from space that reaches Earth's surface

_____ 2. broken pieces of something

_____ 3. hit with force while moving

_____ 4. large dents in Earth's surface caused by big objects hitting it while moving fast.

_____ 5. the Sun and all the planets and other bodies that move around the Sun

_____ 6. to watch or check on regularly over a period of time

_____ 7. space objects made of ice and dust that travel around the Sun

VOCABULARY

Read these words from the passage. Check the words you know.

- [ ] collide
- [ ] comets
- [ ] craters
- [ ] debris
- [ ] meteorite
- [ ] solar system

Functional Vocabulary

- [ ] monitor

© New Readers Press. All rights reserved.

3. Work With New Vocabulary

Write T *if a statement is true. Write* F *if the statement is false and explain why it is false.*

The root *sol* in *solar* means "sun." The root *luna* in *lunar* means "moon."

1. _____ In our **solar system**, the other planets **revolve** around Earth.

   _____

2. _____ An **orbit** is the path an object travels when it falls from Earth's atmosphere to the ground.

   _____

3. _____ An **astronomer** studies objects in space such as stars and planets.

   _____

4. _____ A **crater** is a rock from space that has landed on Earth.

   _____

5. _____ You can only see a **comet** if it crashes to Earth.

   _____

Answer the questions. Explain your answers.

6. How does a **constellation** compare to a **galaxy**?

   _____

The second syllable of *debris* rhymes with *free*. The letter *s* is silent.

7. What does **debris** look like when a building is destroyed or falls down?

   _____

8. If you wanted to **confirm** that your favorite sports team won a game, what would you do?

   _____

9. Are **meteorites** easy to find? Explain your answer.

   _____

10. Why might a scientist need to **magnify** an object?

    _____

11. Do young children need to **monitored**? Explain your answer.

    _____

12. Is it a good thing or a bad thing when two vehicles **collide**? Explain why.

    _____

© New Readers Press. All rights reserved.

4. Prefix trans-

The prefix _trans-_ means "across" or "through." For example, if you _transplant_ a plant, you take it from one place and plant it in another.

Complete each sentence with a word from the list.

transformed	transition	translate	transmits	transparent	transported

1. A rocket _____ or carried the Hubble Space Telescope into orbit.

2. The detailed information that the telescope sent back to Earth has _____, or changed, how scientists view the universe and what they know about it.

3. The Hubble Space Telescope sends information to a satellite. The satellite then _____ the data to a space operations center on Earth.

4. Scientists and computers at the operations center steer the Hubble Telescope and _____ raw data from the telescope into images that people can view.

5. A good time to use a telescope on Earth is after a rainstorm. The sky is more _____ because rain clears away dust and smog.

6. NASA will _____ or change from using the Hubble Space Telescope to using the new James Webb Space Telescope when it is launched later in this decade.

5. Roots astr, aster

The roots _astr_ and _aster_ mean "star." These roots combine with other roots, prefixes, and suffixes to form words. For example, in the word _astronomer_, the root _astr_ (star) is combined with the root _nomos_ (arranging) and the suffix –_er_ (a person who). So an astronomer is a person who studies the stars and planets.

> The Latin root _stella_ also means "star." The words _constellation_ and _stellar_ contain this root.

Match each word to its definition. Write the letter of the correct definition on the line.

_____ 1. astronaut

_____ 2. asterisk

_____ 3. disaster

_____ 4. astronomy

_____ 5. asteroid

_____ 6. astral

a. the study of stars and planets

b. related to the stars or space

c. a small, star-shaped symbol used in printing (*)

d. a person who travels into space

e. a planet-like object that orbits the Sun

f. a bad, unexpected event that causes damage or hurts people

© New Readers Press. All rights reserved.

6. Context Clues: Synonyms and General Clues

Synonyms are words with similar meanings. An author might use a synonym to avoid repeating the same word over and over. If you don't understand a word, check to see if the author uses a synonym that you do know.

Read the passage about satellites. Look for clues to help you understand the meanings of the boldfaced words. Answer the questions.

Notice how the first sentence defines what a satellite is.

A **satellite** is an object that orbits a larger body, such as a planet or a star. Some satellites are natural, like the Moon that orbits Earth. Other satellites are **artificial**, or man-made. We **depend** on satellites for many important tasks. For example, they help predict weather. They are also used for **communications**, including sending TV signals and transmitting phone calls. Other satellites are for **navigation**. The Global Positioning System (GPS) has a group of more than 20 satellites that help people find their exact **locations** on Earth and get directions to other places.

The Soviet Union **launched** the first satellite, *Sputnik 1*, in 1957. A few months later, the U.S. responded when the satellite *Explorer 1* was sent into space. Today there are thousands of satellites orbiting Earth. This has created a problem—space junk. Some satellites are broken. Others have been **abandoned**, meaning no one takes care of them. Satellites and pieces of space junk travel at extreme **velocities**. Their speeds can be 17,000 miles an hour or more. Although **collisions** between satellites are rare, crashes do sometimes happen. For example, in 2009, a Russian and an American satellite collided in space.

1. How does the passage define **satellite**? _____

2. What phrase in the passage means the same as **artificial**? _____

3. What does it mean to **depend on** something? _____

4. What are the examples of **communications**? _____

5. What words in the passage explain what **navigation** is? _____

6. Which word in the passage means about the same as **locations**? _____

7. What words in the passage mean about the same as **launched**? _____

8. What does it mean when objects are **abandoned**? _____

9. Which word means about the same as **velocities**? _____

10. Which word is a synonym for **collisions**? _____

© New Readers Press. All rights reserved.

7. Parts of Speech and the Dictionary

Dictionaries give more information than a word's pronunciation, definition, and part of speech. They also give information about irregular verbs. Irregular verbs do not form the past tense by adding *–d* or *–ed* at the end. For example, if you look up the verb *fly* in the dictionary, you will see that the past tense is *flew*.

Look at each boldfaced word. Circle the part it plays in the sentence. Then look up the word in a dictionary. Write the definition that matches how the word is used in the sentence.

noun   verb   1. Space objects that **strike** Earth can cause damage.

_____

noun   verb   2. A telescope can use lenses and mirrors to **gather** light.

_____

noun   verb   3. Some people get TV signals through a satellite dish. They may need to change the **position** of the dish and aim it to get the best signal.

_____

noun   verb   4. Many small pieces of space **matter** hit Earth every day.

_____

noun   verb   5. Long ago, people used the very bright North Star to **guide** them.

_____

> The verb *strike* is irregular. The past tense of *strike* is *struck*.

8. Multiple-Meaning Words

Many words have more than one meaning. As you read, use context to decide which meaning of a word makes the most sense.

Look at each underlined word. Circle the letter of the best definition.

1. When an object hits Earth's atmosphere, it makes a <u>flash</u> of light.
   a. a device for taking photographs
   b. a sudden bright light

2. Because satellites are in orbit, they can see more of Earth and <u>collect</u> more information than instruments on Earth can.
   a. to get and keep things as a hobby
   b. bring together things from different places

3. A satellite orbits a larger <u>body</u> like a planet.
   a. an object
   b. the main part of a vehicle

4. Scientists monitor the <u>paths</u> of comets and asteroids to make sure they aren't headed toward Earth.
   a. plans of action
   b. the lines along which something moves

5. Devices like cell phones use GPS satellite data to give people <u>directions</u> to get to specific places.
   a. instructions about where to go
   b. the paths on which something moves

> When you look up words with multiple meanings in the dictionary, first find the correct part of speech. Then look for a definition that makes sense for the topic you are reading about.

© New Readers Press. All rights reserved.

Unit 12 Review

Complete each sentence with a word from the list.

asterisks	collision	comets	debris	flash	galaxies

1. Some _____ can take 4,000 years to make one complete trip around the Sun. It's a big event when these objects can be seen from Earth.

2. In the 1920s, Edwin Hubble used a telescope with a 100-inch mirror to study space. He discovered that there are many _____ beyond our own.

3. The _____ in orbit around Earth includes pieces of broken satellites, parts of used rockets, and nuts and bolts.

4. NASA scientists worry about what will happen if there is a _____ between spacecraft and some of the space junk in Earth's orbit.

5. A meteor is the _____ of light we see when a piece of space matter burns up in Earth's atmosphere.

6. _____ are shaped like stars.

Choose the best word to complete each sentence. Write it on the line.

7. Telescopes are useful tools for astronomers because they can _____ objects that are very far away or that appear small.

    gather   **launch**   **magnify**

8. Rockets _____ satellites into orbit around Earth.

    transport   **translate**   **transform**

9. A large _____ hit Arizona about 50,000 years ago. The impact formed a crater about 4,000 feet wide and 600 feet deep.

    solar system   **constellation**   **meteorite**

10. In 1969, NASA sent three _____ to the Moon. Neil Armstrong was the first human to walk on the Moon.

    astronomers   **astronauts**   **satellites**

How has what we know about space changed over time? How has knowledge about space helped people in the past and present? Write your answer on a separate sheet of paper. Use at least five words you learned in this unit. Circle the vocabulary words you use.

© New Readers Press. All rights reserved.

TESTING TIP:

When you read a test question, pay attention to key words. Make sure you understand what the question asks. Here are some examples of types of vocabulary questions. The keywords are in italics:

- What is the *meaning* or *definition* of a word?
- Which meaning *matches how a word is used* in a passage?
- Which word is a *synonym* or has the *same meaning* as another word?

Circle the letter of the correct answer.

1. **What is the meaning of the word *orbit*?**

    A a group of stars that forms a shape in the sky

    B the curved path that an object travels as it moves around a larger object

    C an object in space that travels around another object

    D a bowl-shaped hole on the surface of Earth formed by an object hitting the ground

2. **Which word best completes the passage?**

    In the past, people used groups of stars for _____. On the open sea, for example, stars could help people understand where they were and where they were going.

    A communications

    B velocities

    C navigation

    D astronomy

3. **Which of the following is an example of something that is *transparent*?**

    A a glass window

    B a man-made satellite

    C an asteroid

    D a piece of wood

4. **Which meaning of *monitor* matches how the word is used in this sentence?**

    Scientists <u>monitor</u> the paths of objects in our solar system to see if any are likely to hit Earth.

    A a screen used with a computer

    B a person whose job is to watch over an activity

    C to secretly listen to someone's phone calls

    D to watch and check something over time

5. **What does *strike* mean in this sentence?**

    When large objects from space <u>strike</u> Earth, they can cause a lot of damage.

    A fall from

    B circle

    C hit

    D pass by

6. **What word in the passage means about the same as *velocities*?**

    Satellites travel at high <u>velocities</u> around Earth. They can reach 17,500 miles per hour. Even small marble-sized pieces of space junk could cause damage at those speeds.

    A satellites

    B miles

    C pieces

    D speeds

Check your answers on page 108.

© New Readers Press. All rights reserved.

Answer Key

UNIT 1

Exercise 1, p. 8
1. prepare
2. acquired
3. continent
4. expedition
5. explore
6. identify
7. territory

Exercise 2, p. 9
1. specimens
2. observations
3. described
4. geography
5. journey
6. labeled
7. region

Exercise 3, p. 10
Explanations will vary.
1. F
2. F
3. F
4. T
5. F
6. T
7. F
8.–12. Answers will vary.

Exercise 4, p. 11
1. procure
2. protect
3. provided
4. proceed
5. produced
6.–7. Sentences will vary.

Exercise 5, p. 11
1. e   4. f
2. a   5. b
3. c   6. d

Exercise 6, p. 12
1.–6. Answers will vary.
7. supplies
8. saved
9. chose
10. large numbers

Exercise 7, p. 13
1. noun
2. adjective
3. adjective
4. noun
5. verb
Definitions will vary.

Exercise 8, p. 13
1. b   4. b
2. a   5. b
3. a

Review, p. 14
1. b
2. c
3. b
4. a
5. provisions
6. route
7. acquired
8. procured

Review, p. 15
1. A   4. C
2. A   5. D
3. D   6. B

UNIT 2

Exercise 1, p. 16
1. slavery
2. abolitionists
3. labor
4. plantations
5. secede
6. opposed
7. preserve

Exercise 2, p. 17
1. border
2. battle
3. wounded
4. defeat
5. invade
6. dedication
7. surrender

Exercise 3, p. 18
Answers will vary.

Exercise 4, p. 19
1. Union
2. unify
3. unique
4. united
5. University

Exercise 5, p. 19
1. access
2. exceeded
3. preceded
4. secede
5. proceed
6. successful

Exercise 6, p. 20
Definitions will vary

Exercise 7, p. 21
1. noun
2. noun
3. noun
4. verb
5. adjective
Definitions will vary.

Exercise 8, p. 21
1. a   3. b
2. a   4. a

Review, p. 22
1. Abolitionists, opposed
2. preserve, seceded
3. troops, surrender

4. labor, industrialized
5. a
6. b
7. b
8. a

Review, p. 23
1. C   4. B
2. C   5. C
3. A   6. A

UNIT 3

Exercise 1, p. 24
1. immigration
2. citizen
3. famine
4. settle
5. majority
6. freedom
7. persecution

Exercise 2, p. 25
1. prejudice
2. inspections
3. legal
4. port
5. detained
6. rise
7. limited

Exercise 3, p. 26
Answers will vary.

Exercise 4, p. 27
1. antisocial
2. anti-democratic
3. antislavery
4. antiwar
5. anti-immigrant

Exercise 5, p. 27
1. emigrants
2. migrants
3. migrate
4. emigrate

© New Readers Press. All rights reserved.

5. migration
6. migratory

Exercise 6, p. 28
1. journey
2. Approximately
3. reunited
4. admitted
5.–8. Definitions will vary.

Exercise 7, p. 29
1. noun
2. adjective
3. verb
4. verb
5. adjective
Definitions will vary.

Exercise 8, p. 29
1. b
2. b
3. b
4. b

Review, p. 30
1. c
2. a
3. a
4. b
5. reunited
6. ancestors
7. pass
8. destination

Review, p. 31
1. C
2. D
3. C
4. A
5. A
6. B

UNIT 4

Exercise 1, p. 32
1. extended
2. guaranteed
3. proposed
4. amendment
5. suffrage
6. convention
7. ratified

Exercise 2, p. 33
1. demonstrations
2. reform
3. civil disobedience
4. organized
5. movement
6. protested
7. debate

Exercise 3, p. 34
Answers will vary.

Exercise 4, p. 35
1. commander
2. amended
3. mandatory
4. demands
5. reprimanded
6. recommend

Exercise 5, p. 35
1. migration
2. organization
3. protection
4. separation
5. demonstration
6. introduction
7.–9. Definitions will vary.

Exercise 6, p. 36
Definitions will vary.

Exercise 7, p. 37
1. verb
2. verb
3. verb
4. noun
5. noun
Definitions will vary.

Exercise 8, p. 37
1. b
2. a
3. b
4. a

Review, p. 38
1. b
2. c
3. a

4. b
5. civil disobedience
6. convention
7. ratified
8. debate

Review, p. 39
1. C
2. B
3. A
4. C
5. D
6. C

UNIT 5

Exercise 1, p. 40
1. prosperity
2. consumers
3. effects
4. unemployment
5. income
6. economy
7. depression

Exercise 2, p. 41
1. expanded
2. crisis
3. Production
4. Recovery
5. debt
6. policies
7. relief

Exercise 3, p. 42
Explanations will vary.
1. F
2. T
3. F
4. F
5. F
6. F
7. T
8. T
9.–12. Answers will vary.

Exercise 4, p. 43
1. b
2. d
3. f
4. e
5. a
6. c

Exercise 5, p. 43
1. investments
2. unemployment
3. achievement

4. environment
5. government
6. development
7. improvement

Exercise 6, p. 44
Definitions will vary.

Exercise 7, p. 45
1. noun
2. adjective
3. verb
4. adjective
5. adjective
Definitions will vary.

Exercise 8, p. 45
1. b
2. b
3. b
4. a
5. a

Review, p. 46
1. government
2. program
3. produced
4. rural
5. expanded
6. native
7. express
8. crash
9. income

Review, p. 47
1. D
2. B
3. A
4. C
5. C
6. B

UNIT 6

Exercise 1, p. 48
1. prevent
2. source
3. generate
4. unreliable
5. hydroelectric power
6. irrigate
7. annual

© New Readers Press. All rights reserved.

Exercise 2, p. 49

1. variety
2. schedule
3. habitats
4. residents
5. primary
6. reservoir
7. budget

Exercise 3, p. 50

Answers will vary.

Exercise 4, p. 51

1. Midwest
2. midterm
3. midtown
4. mid-1930s
5. mid-August
6. Midway

Exercise 5, p. 51

1. affordable
2. possible
3. profitable
4. changeable
5. comparable
6. visible
7.–9. Definitions will vary.

Exercise 6, p. 52

Definitions will vary.

Exercise 7, p. 53

1. verb
2. noun
3. verb
4. verb
5. noun

Definitions will vary.

Exercise 8, p. 53

1. b   3. a
2. b   4. a

Review, p. 54

1. desolate
2. foundation

3. massive
4. irrigates
5. habitat
6. a
7. c
8. c
9. b

Review, p. 55

1. B   4. D
2. B   5. A
3. A   6. C

UNIT 7

Exercise 1, p. 56

1. precipitation
2. vegetation
3. climate
4. defined
5. survive
6. species
7. biome

Exercise 2, p. 57

1. composition
2. similar
3. concluded
4. adapted
5. ecosystem
6. theory
7. evolution

Exercise 3, p. 58

Answers will vary.

Exercise 4, p. 59

2. cardiologist
3. zoology
4. Anthropology
5. biologist
6. geology
7. Dermatology

Exercise 5, p. 59

1. nocturnal
2. tropical
3. annual

4. national
5. seasonal
6. natural

Exercise 6, p. 60

Answers will vary.

Exercise 7, p. 61

1. noun
2. noun
3. adjective
4. verb
5. adjective

Definitions will vary.

Exercise 8, p. 61

1. a   4. b
2. b   5. a
3. a

Review, p. 62

1. b
2. b
3. c
4. c
5. ecosystem
6. extinct
7. survive
8. natural

Review, p. 63

1. A   4. B
2. D   5. A
3. C   6. C

UNIT 8

Exercise 1, p. 64

1. innate
2. combine
3. Mammals
4. flexible
5. Predators
6. interact
7. predictable

Exercise 2, p. 65

1. signal

2. visual
3. imitating
4. comprehend
5. specialized
6. role
7. exhibit

Exercise 3, p. 66

Explanations will vary.

1. F
2. F
3. F
4. T
5. F
6. F
7. F
8.–14. Answers will vary.

Exercise 4, p. 67

1. construct
2. complicated
3. compete
4. coexist
5.–7. Answers will vary.

Exercise 5, p. 67

1. e   4. b
2. d   5. f
3. a   6. c

Exercise 6, p. 68

Definitions will vary.

Exercise 7, p. 69

1. adjective
2. noun
3. noun
4. noun
5. adjective

Definitions will vary.

Exercise 8, p. 69

1. b
2. a
3. a
4. b
5. a

© New Readers Press. All rights reserved.

Review, p. 70
1. signals, attract
2. roles, cooperate
3. flexible, adapt
4. mammals, imitating
5. coexist, compete
6. b
7. a
8. a
9. c

Review, p. 71
1. A   4. B
2. A   5. A
3. C   6. D

UNIT 9

Exercise 1, p. 72
1. compress
2. gradual
3. created
4. elevations
5. glacier
6. erode
7. dense

Exercise 2, p. 73
1. particles
2. classify
3. pollution
4. erupt
5. vents
6. pressure
7. landforms

Exercise 3, p. 74
Answers will vary.

Exercise 4, p. 75
1. f   4. c
2. e   5. a
3. b   6. d

Exercise 5, p. 75
Sentences will vary.

Exercise 6, p. 76
Sentences will vary.

Exercise 7, p. 77
1. noun
2. verb
3. adjective
4. verb
5. noun
Definitions will vary.

Exercise 8, p. 77
1. b   4. b
2. a   5. a
3. b

Review, p. 78
1. a
2. c
3. b
4. c
5. explosive
6. store
7. smooth
8. compress
9. sediment

Review, p. 79
1. C   4. D
2. B   5. C
3. D   6. A

UNIT 10

Exercise 1, p. 80
1. wildfires
2. fuel
3. humidity
4. destroy
5. embers
6. occur
7. flammable

Exercise 2, p. 81
1. approach
2. collapse
3. storm surge

4. scale
5. coastal
6. categorize
7. rotate

Exercise 3, p. 82
Explanations will vary.
1. F
2. T
3. F
4. F
5. F
6. F
7.–12. Answers will vary

Exercise 4, p. 83
Sentences will vary.

Exercise 5, p. 83
1. probability
2. activity
3. ability
4. similarity
5. majority
6. equality
7. security

Exercise 6, p. 84
Definitions will vary.

Exercise 7, p. 85
1. verb
2. noun
3. noun
4. adjective
5. verb
Definitions will vary.

Exercise 8, p. 85
1. a   4. b
2. a   5. b
3. b

Review, p. 86
1. occur
2. categorize
3. approaches

4. moisture
5. renew
6. glaze
7. certainty
8. cover
9. severe
10. evidence

Review, p. 87
1. C   4. D
2. A   5. B
3. B   6. D

UNIT 11

Exercise 1, p. 88
1. cycles
2. meteorologists
3. atmosphere
4. data
5. varies
6. predict
7. direct

Exercise 2, p. 89
1. sustained
2. reverse
3. mild
4. phenomenon
5. impact
6. Circulation
7. mass

Exercise 3, p. 90
1.–7. Answers will vary.
Explanations will vary.
8. F   12. T
9. F   13. F
10. F   14. F
11. F

Exercise 4, p. 91
1. c   4. a
2. d   5. f
3. b   6. e

© New Readers Press. All rights reserved.

Exercise 5, p. 91

1. specific
2. volcanic
3. public
4. problematic
5. economic
6. academic

Exercise 6, p. 92

Definitions will vary.

Exercise 7, p. 93

1. verb
2. noun
3. adjective
4. noun
5. noun

Definitions will vary.

Exercise 8, p. 93

1. b   4. b
2. a   5. b
3. b

Review, p. 94

1. economic
2. extreme
3. Sustained
4. circulates
5. data
6. a
7. b

8. a
9. a

Review, p. 95

1. C   4. B
2. C   5. D
3. B   6. A

UNIT 12

Exercise 1, p. 96

1. confirm
2. magnify
3. astronomers
4. orbit
5. Galaxies
6. revolve
7. constellations

Exercise 2, p. 97

1. meteorite
2. debris
3. collide
4. craters
5. solar system
6. monitor
7. comets

Exercise 3, p. 98

Explanations will vary.

1. F
2. F

3. T
4. F
5. F
6.–12. Answers will vary.

Exercise 4, p. 99

1. transported
2. transformed
3. transmits
4. translate
5. transparent
6. transition

Exercise 5, p. 99

1. d   4. a
2. c   5. e
3. f   6. b

Exercise 6, p. 100

1. an object that orbits a larger body
2. man-made
3. Answers will vary.
4. TV signals and phone calls
5. find exact locations, get directions
6. places
7. sent into space
8. no one takes care of them

9. speeds
10. crashes

Exercise 7, p. 101

1. verb
2. verb
3. noun
4. noun
5. verb

Definitions will vary.

Exercise 8, p. 101

1. b   4. b
2. b   5. a
3. a

Review, p. 102

1. comets
2. galaxies
3. debris
4. collision
5. flash
6. Asterisks
7. magnify
8. transport
9. meteorite
10. astronauts

Review, p. 103

1. B   4. D
2. C   5. C
3. A   6. D

© New Readers Press. All rights reserved.

Appendix I: Common Prefixes

Prefix	Meaning	Example
anti-	against, opposite of	antibiotic antihero
circ- **circum-**	around, about	circle circumference
co- **com-** **con-**	together, with	coexist compete construct
de-	opposite, down	decrease
dis-	not, opposite of	disagree
em- en-	cause to	employer endanger
ex-	out of, from	explode
fore-	before	foresee
il- in- im- ir-	not, opposite of	illegal indirect impossible irresponsible
in- im-	in or into	invite immigrate
inter-	among, between	interact
mid-	middle	midnight
mis-	wrongly	misspeak
multi-	many	multiple
non-	not, opposite of	nonsense
over-	too much, above	overreact
pre-	before	preview
pro-	in front of, before, for, forward	protect
re-	again, back	restart
semi-	half	semicircle
sub-	under, lower	subtitle
super-	above, beyond	supermarket
trans-	across	transmit
un-	not, opposite of	unhappy
uni-	one	uniform
under-	too little, below	underrated underground

Prefixes in **boldface** are discussed in this book.

© New Readers Press. All rights reserved.

Appendix II: Common Suffixes

Suffix	Meaning	Example
-able **-ible**	is, can be	manageable possible
-al -ial	having characteristics of	natural financial
-ed	past form of verbs	wanted
-en	made of	wooden
-er	comparative	longer
-er -or	one who	researcher inventor
-est	superlative	deepest
-ful	full of	careful
-ic	having characteristics of	scientific
-ing	present participle	speaking
-ion **-tion** **-ation**	the act or process of doing something	migration demonstration organization
-ist	one who practices	chemist
-ity	state of	activity
-ive -ative -itive	adjective form of a noun	decisive informative repetitive
-less	without	worthless
-logy **-logist**	study of; person who studies	biology geologist
-ly	characteristic of	happily
-ment	action or process	government
-ness	state of, condition of	awareness
-ous -eous -ious	possessing the qualities of	dangerous righteous serious
-s -es	plural	books boxes
-y	characterized by	noisy

Suffixes in **boldface** are taught in this book.

© New Readers Press. All rights reserved.

Appendix III: Common Roots

Root	Meaning	Example
act **ag**	do, act	activity agenda
astr **aster**	star	astronomy asteroid
audi	hear	audience
auto	self	automobile
bene bon boun	good, well	benefit bonus bountiful
bio	life	biology
cede ceed cess	go	precede proceeds success
cycle	circle	recycle
dic dict	say	dedicate predict
duc duct	make, lead	produce conduct
geo	earth	geography
graph	write	paragraph
jur jus	law	jury justice
mand **mend**	order	command recommend
meter metr	measure	perimeter geometry
migr	move	immigrants
phon	sound	telephone
port	carry	transport
pos	place	deposit
press	to force, squeeze, press	express
scrib script	write	scribble prescription
spec	to look; to watch	inspect
tele	far off	telescope
therm	heat	thermometer
val	worth, strength, health	evaluate
vid **vis**	see, look at	evidence vision

Roots in **boldface** are taught in this book.

© New Readers Press. All rights reserved.

Personal Dictionary

Create your own dictionary. Write down any words you want to remember.

Word	Definition	Used in a Sentence	Notes

© New Readers Press. All rights reserved.